THE PRINCIPAL'S GUIDE TO

SCHOOL BUDGETING

THE PRINCIPAL'S GUIDE TO

SCHOOL BUDGETING

RICHARD D. SORENSON   LLOYD MILTON GOLDSMITH

CORWIN PRESS
A SAGE Publications Company
Thousand Oaks, California

For information:

Corwin Press
A Sage Publications Company
2455 Teller Road
Thousand Oaks, California 91320
www.corwinpress.com

Sage Publications Ltd.
1 Oliver's Yard
55 City Road
London EC1Y 1SP
United Kingdom

Sage Publications India Pvt. Ltd.
B-42, Panchsheel Enclave
Post Box 4109
New Delhi 110 017 India

Printed in the United States of America.

Library of Congress Cataloging-in-Publication Data

Sorenson, Richard D.
The principal's guide to school budgeting / Richard D. Sorenson,
Lloyd Milton Goldsmith.
    p. cm.
Includes bibliographical references and index.
ISBN 978-1-4129-2531-0 (cloth) — ISBN 978-1-4129-2532-7 (pbk.)
    1. School budgets—United States. I. Goldsmith, Lloyd Milton. II. Title.
LB2830.2.S67 2006
371.2'060973—dc22

2005031712

This book is printed on acid-free paper.

08   09   10   9   8   7   6   5   4   3

Acquisitions Editor:	Elizabeth Brenkus
Editorial Assistant:	Desirée Enayati
Production Editor:	Jenn Reese
Copy Editor:	Marjorie Cappellari
Typesetter:	C&M Digitals (P) Ltd.
Proofreader:	Penelope Sippel
Indexer:	Judy Hunt
Cover Designer:	Rose Storey
Graphic Designer:	Lisa Miller

Contents

Preface

Effective practice in school administration is continuously being redefined by reform movements and initiatives such as state deregulation, district decentralization, school restructuring, and other organizational modifications and transformations. These ever-changing practices, to include the most recently passed No Child Left Behind Act of 2001, bring into question the roles and expectations associated with being a modern-day school leader. How will the next generation of educational leaders be prepared for the "real world" of school administration?

The Principal's Guide to School Budgeting is purposefully written for practicing and aspiring public and private school administrators who want to enhance their instructional, technical, and managerial skills not only as the school's leader but also as the school's visionary, planning coordinator, and budgeting manager. The authors provide the reader with an essential understanding of the interwoven relationship between two independent yet distinctly connected accountability systems—academic and fiscal.

School leaders—from a financial and budgetary perspective—are responsible for understanding the equity issues and fiscal consequences associated with school budgeting as well as the relationship between educational goal development and resource allocation management. The authors provide school leaders with an overview of school budgeting practices within a collaborative decision-making context. Using school-oriented situations and the national standards for administrators as they relate to school leadership and budgeting, the reader acquires the necessary skills to plan and develop a budget, allocate, expend and monitor funds, manage and evaluate budget reports, and prepare school action plans aligned with a fiscal accountability system.

To enhance the book's usefulness as a desk resource, it has been purposely organized into brief, single-topic-focused chapters. Each chapter begins with an appropriate quote and general overview, and includes numerous visuals, tables, and relevant activities such as utilizing accounting codes, projecting student populations, conducting a needs assessment, implementing a budget calendar, and building, defending, and amending a budget. For example:

Chapters 1, *Understanding the Budgeting Process*, examines the delineation between school finance and school budgeting, the basics of school finance, sources of school funding, and steps to budgetary success.

Chapter 2, *The Budget-Vision Relationship and the National Standards*, presents and reviews the Educational Leadership Constituent Council (ELCC) and the Interstate School Leaders Licensure Consortium (ISLLC) standards in relation to the correlation between budget, vision, and planning, knowledge, and skills necessary to be an effective school leader, and the three keys to ethics in school leadership.

Chapter 3, *School Culture and Using Data Effectively*, reflects upon the importance of school culture, data-driven decision making, and types of data and assessment as related to academic planning and school budgeting.

Chapter 4, *A Model for Integrating Vision, Planning, and Budgeting*, showcases an eight-component model related to budget and vision implementation and concludes with a "real life" planning metaphor which correlates with the elements of an educational action plan.

Chapter 5, *Effective and Efficient Budgeting Practices*, examines the budget plan, expenditure accountability and control, budgetary systems, and accounting and auditing procedures. The No Child Left Behind Act of 2001 (NCLB) is examined in relation to the numerous dictates, such as high quality teachers and schools in need of assistance, each of which are central to the act, and just as important from a budgetary perspective, cost money—money that school districts often do not have.

Chapter 6, *Building the School Budget*, reflects upon the budgeting process and those responsible for building the budget, coding applications, the concept of projecting student enrollment, and major budgeting issues and considerations.

Chapter 7, *Celebrating Success, Acknowledging Opportunities, and Ethical Leadership*, permits the reader to contemplate the issues of celebrating success, acknowledging opportunities for professional growth and development, and modeling ethical and moral behaviors in the leadership role.

Special features of the book include:

- Discussion questions
- Case Study applications and problems
- Experiential exercises
- Budgeting Checklist for administrators
- Selected templates and forms
- References and resources

School budgeting is a daunting process for many school leaders because most are not bookkeepers, accountants, or financial planners. Many have received minimal training in the budgeting process. This process involves not only computerized accounting procedures and programs, but vision and goal development, instructional planning, and decision making. This can intimidate even the best educational leaders due to their lack of understanding of school-based budgeting and its integrative approaches. Such can explain the willingness of some leaders to ignore, avoid, or pass on certain budgetary and planning responsibilities to others. For these reasons alone, *The Principal's Guide to School Budgeting,* has been written by two former school administrators with a combined 60 years of experience in the public school arena and who, moreover, have extensive practical experience working with site-based decision making committees in writing instructional goals and objectives, in the development of school and district budgets, and in defending instructional and budget outcomes to superintendents and school boards.

The Principal's Guide to School Budgeting is not designed to be an exhaustive study of the budget and planning subject nor is it designed to merely provide a basic understanding of the topic. Instead, the contents provide the necessary information and tools needed to incorporate the ideas set forth into real school applications. As a result, readers will be able to take the integrated budget, vision, and planning concepts presented and incorporate them in a practical and relevant manner in their own school settings.

Acknowledgments

We would like to express our appreciation to several individuals who contributed to the development of our book, *The Principal's Guide to School Budgeting*. So many people have influenced our lives and careers as school administrators and university professors. To those special individuals and friends we publicly extend our respect and gratitude. A special acknowledgment is extended to the fine folks at Corwin Press, especially Lizzie Brenkus, who believed in us and took our written project and helped us fulfill another goal in our professional lives.

First, I would like to thank my spouse and children: Donna, my loving wife, my best friend, and the mother of my two children—Lisa (hook 'em horns) and Ryan (God has His hands on you). Second, this book has been strengthened by the contributions of my dear friend and former colleague—Alice Frick, school finance wizard, extraordinaire—and Adriana E. Spencer, UTEP graduate student and research assistant. Both of these individuals provided invaluable advice and assistance. For allowing me to try out all of my budgeting "stuff," a special note of appreciation is extended to the graduate students in the Department of Educational Leadership and Foundations at The University of Texas at El Paso. Finally, thanks Mom and Dad for your love and support, and for always being there.

—RDS

I would like to thank Mary, my patient wife and confidant, for having patience with me through this process. To my three children Abigail, Eleanor, and Nelson, I say thank you for just being the neat kids that you are. No, you don't have to read the book. I want to thank my colleagues, Dr. Donnie Snider and Dr. Jerry Whitworth, for their invaluable support and advice. A special thanks to Jeff Strickland, a beginning administrator, for his opinions and comments as the manuscript was being developed. Finally, thanks to Bob and Montie Spaulding for being spiritual advisors to me for most of my life, helping me to keep first things first.

—LMG

Publisher's Acknowledgments

Corwin Press gratefully acknowledges the contributions of the following individuals:

Steve Zsiray
Associate Superintendent of Curriculum and Instruction
Cache County School District
North Logan, UT

Glenn Sewell
Superintendent/Principal
Wheatland Union High School District
Wheatland, CA

Jane L. Sigford
Executive Director of Curriculum and Instruction
Corwin Author
Wayzata Public Schools
Wayzata, MN

Darin Drill
Principal
Cascade High School
Turner, OR

About the Authors

 **Richard D. Sorenson** is an assistant professor in the Educational Leadership and Foundations Department at The University of Texas at El Paso. He received his EdD from Texas A&M University at Corpus Christi in the area of educational leadership. Dr. Sorenson served public schools for 25 years as a social studies teacher, principal, and assistant superintendent of instruction and personnel. Currently, Dr. Sorenson works with graduate students at UTEP in the area of educational law, personnel, school-based budgeting, and leadership development. He has most recently been named The University of Texas at El Paso College of Education Teacher of the Year (2005), and he is an active writer with numerous professional journal publications. Dr. Sorenson has also authored textbooks, teacher resource guides, and workbooks in the area of the elementary and secondary social studies curricula. He conducts workshops at the state and national levels on topics such as instructional leadership and effective teaching practices, and he has been actively involved in numerous professional organizations including the Texas Elementary Principals and Supervisors Association (TEPSA), the Texas Association of Secondary School Principals (TASSP), and the Texas Council for the Social Studies (TCSS). Dr. Sorenson's research interest is in the area of the school principalship, specifically the examination of conditions and factors that inhibit and discourage lead teachers from entering school administration. He has been married to his wife, Donna, for the past 30 years, and has two children—Lisa and Ryan, all of whom are the pride and joy of his life.

 **Lloyd Milton Goldsmith** earned his EdD in educational leadership from Baylor University. Currently he is an assistant professor in the Education Department at Abilene Christian University where he also serves as the Director of the Graduate Education Program. Dr. Goldsmith teaches educational law and instructional leadership. He served public schools for 29 years as an elementary science teacher, middle school assistant principal, and elementary school principal. He and a fellow chemistry professor co-direct a program to facilitate high school chemistry teachers in developing effective instructional strategies. He also serves on the Higher Education Collaborative at The University of Texas at Austin. This initiative assists principals and superintendents in developing a greater understanding of reading instruction. Dr. Goldsmith has served on several state committees for the Texas Education Agency. His research interest relates to issues faced by school districts with less than 500 students. Dr. Goldsmith has been married to his wife, Mary, for the past 20 years and has three children—Abigail, Eleanor, and Nelson all of whom give meaning to his life.

*Dedicated to Louise Moser and Xavier Barrera
who helped shape us into effective school leaders.*

—the Boys

1

Understanding the Budgeting Process

A budget will not work unless you do!

—Anonymous

The Basics of School Budgeting

Whether we recognize it or not, school leaders devote a vast amount of time and energy to school funding and budgeting issues. Those leaders who fail to do so commit a terrible disservice to their school and, more important, to their students. Why is budgeting so essential beyond the stated reason? First and foremost, the budgeting process enables school leaders to develop an understanding of the need for strong organizational skills and technical competence. Recall that numerous studies have documented the importance of strong organizational skills to an individual's success and effectiveness as a leader. Hughes, et al. (2002) reveal that technical competence concerns the knowledge base and particular behaviors that one can bring to successfully completing a task. School leaders generally acquire technical competence, specifically in relation to the budgetary process, through formal education or training, but more often than not, it comes from on-the-job experiences (Yukl, 2001). Thus, one can readily note that one of the primary purposes of this book is to effectively serve as a school leader's guide to appropriate and effective school-based budgeting.

Knowing how to properly develop a budget for a school and recognizing why budgeting and accounting procedures are an integral part of an instructional program are keys to understanding why goal development and instructional planning are significantly impacted by the budgeting process. Appropriation of public funds for a school is ensured by adopting a budget that includes all estimated revenues and proposed expenditures for a 12-month fiscal year. Budget accounts in most states are reported electronically under a Fiscal Education Information Management System (FEIMS). The FEIMS process will be examined in greater detail in Chapter 5. Therefore, the adoption of a district budget by the local school board provides the legal authorization for school leaders to expend public funds.

The nationally recognized and designated Governmental Accounting Standards Board (GASB) prescribes that budgets for public education entities be reported on the basis of a standard operating accounting code structure (Fowler, 1990). An example of a state's operating accounting code structure is shown by fund, function, object, sub-object, organization, fiscal year, and program intent code in Table 1.1. Most states require that a standard operating accounting code structure be adopted by every school district. A major purpose of the accounting code structure is to ensure that the sequence of codes is uniformly applied to all school districts to further account for the appropriation and expenditure of public funds (Governmental Accounting Standards Board, 2001). This aspect of the budgeting process will be further explored in Chapter 5 as well.

Table 1.1   Example of a State's Operating Accounting Code Structure

199 — 11 — 6399.00 — 001 — 08 — 11

1	2	3	4	5	6	7

1 = Fund Code. *How will the expenditure be financed?*

School district accounting systems are organized and operated on a fund basis. A fund is an accounting entity with a self-balancing set of accounts recording financial resources and liabilities. There are more than 500 different types of fund codes, and examples include: General Fund, Bilingual Education, Title I, Vocational Education, etc.

2 = Function Code. *Why is the expenditure being made?*

The function code is an accounting entity that is applied to expenditures and expenses and identifies the purpose of any school district transaction. There are at least 27 different types of function codes; examples include: Instruction, School Leadership, Guidance Counseling, Health Services, etc.

3 = Object Code. *What is being purchased?*

The object code is an accounting entity identifying the nature and object of an account, a transaction, or a source. There are more than 35 different types of object codes and examples include: Payroll, Professional and Contracted Services, Supplies and Materials, Capital Outlay, etc.

4 = Sub-Object Code. *For which department or grade level is the purchase being made?*

The sub-object code is an accounting entity that is often utilized to delineate, as an example, secondary-level departments.

5 = Organization Code. *What unit is making the purchase?*

The organization code is an accounting entity that identifies the organization, i.e., High School, Middle School, Elementary School, Superintendent's office, etc. The activity, not the location, defines the organization within a school district. There are more than 900 organization codes. For example, expenditures for a high school might be classified as 001 as the organization code for high school campuses are generally identified as 001-040. Middle School organization codes are typically stipulated as 041 through 100. Elementary schools fall into the organization code range of 101-698.

6 = Fiscal Year Code. *During what year is the purchase being made?*

The fiscal year code identifies the fiscal year of any budgetary transaction. For the 2007-2008 fiscal year of a school district, the numeral 08 would denote the fiscal year.

7 = Program Intent Code. *To what student group is the instructional purchase or service being directed?*

The program intent code is used to designate the rationale of a program that is provided to students. These codes are used to account for the cost of instruction and other services that are directed toward a particular need of a specific set of students. There are approximately a dozen program intent codes; examples include: Basic Educational Services, Gifted and Talented, Career and Technology, Special Education, Bilingual Education, Title I Services, etc.

NOTE: The reference numbers used in Table 1.1 were presented by the National Center for Education Statistics and the Governmental Accounting Standards Board in 1990 and revised in 1995. These coded numbers are representative numbers often assigned to state operating accounting code structures.

School leaders at some point in time, typically early in their careers, come to the realization that setting goals, establishing measurable objectives, developing action plans, incorporating the entire learning community in a participatory process, and making student enrollment projections are essential components in the development and implementation of an effective school budget. School administrators must recognize that it is not mere coincidence that the budget planning and development process coincides with the instructional or school action planning process. Both processes are essential to the overall success of any school or, for that matter, any school administrator (Brimley & Garfield, 2002). These two processes must be developed in an integrated approach to achieve the maximum benefits for schools and students. (See Chapter 4.) A school budget must have as its foundation the academic or action plan that details all of the educational programs and initiatives of a school. Such plans must be consistent with the school's vision or mission. Each program, initiative, and activity within an academic or action plan dictate how appropriate budgetary decision-making, as related to funding appropriations and levels, will occur and how it will ultimately impact student achievement.

Breaking the Budgeting Myths

Many instructional leaders begin their careers with several mythical notions related to the budgeting process. The reason or reasons for such thinking may simply relate to the role of leader. Numerous myths have been readily associated with leadership and have been further documented in related research (Hughes, et al., 2002). For example, one leadership myth that is most applicable to the budgetary process stipulates: *Leaders are born, not made.* While certain natural talents or characteristics may provide some individuals with advantages over others, one's training and experiences can play a crucial role in the development of leadership abilities, traits, and skills. This is especially true when one considers that most school leaders have limited knowledge about finance and budgeting but quickly realize that they must build upon their limited skills. Interestingly, several school-based budgeting myths quickly come to mind. These myths often serve to further complicate the budgeting process and can, in fact, serve to disengage a school leader from monitoring and managing an important, if not a critical, aspect of the education business—the school budget. Listed below are ten myths that are often experienced by and associated with school leaders and the school-based budgeting process (Sorenson & Goldsmith, 2004).

1. School leaders must have an analytical mindset.

2. School leaders must have an accounting background or degree.

3. Budgeting, like any fiscal accounting procedure, is too difficult.

4. Educators are "right-brained" and as a result would rather create than compute.

5. Budgeting is for the site-based decision making team to figure out.

6. Physical school-site inventories have little to do with the budgeting process.

7. Instruction and curriculum are more important.

8. School leaders simply do not have the time to meet the demands and dictates associated with the school budget.

9. Central administration retains most of the money anyway.

10. District business managers do not care about or understand the fiscal needs of individual schools.

Few factors can pose a greater obstacle to the school leader than unsubstantiated and self-limiting beliefs or myths about the budgeting process. We argue that by acknowledging and then avoiding these myths, the school leader is provided with the basis for better understanding, developing and handling a school budget. We believe that while these myths are unfortunately prevalent in the world of school administration, recognition of said myths also provide school leaders—particularly novice administrators—with insights that allow for the development of those essential skills to successfully emerge as effective managers of school-based budgets. Remember, being able to recognize and analyze your own experiences in terms of the budgeting myths may be one of the single greatest contributions that this text can provide.

Delineating Between School Finance and School Budgeting

School business has become big business in recent years. Many school districts across the nation are by far the largest enterprises in their communities in terms of revenues, expenditures, employment, and capital assets. Unfortunately, as school leaders we often fail to understand the basis for funding public schools and, as a result, become a victim of our own demise by failing to recognize the financial challenges that are often associated with being a fiscal leader in a big business. What we often fail to understand is the fundamentals associated with school budgeting. In far too many instances, we have limited background, experience, or expertise with the budgeting process as related to the fiscal management of our schools. This dilemma is further complicated by the fact that as school leaders many of us have an inadequate understanding of the basic delineation between school finance and school budgeting.

School finance is often regulated by state and federal legislation, as well as by the courts. All of these have initiated, by law, stringent policies and procedures to infuse greater accountability through the development of financial plans and reports as related to a process that records, classifies, and summarizes fiscal transactions and provides for an accounting of the monetary operations and activities of a school district (Garner, 2004). School finance is most assuredly a concern for superintendents, district business managers, and school board members because the adequacy and equity of state and federal funding is the fiscal lifeline of a school district. However, this book is not about school finance. Our study will be from the perspective of the school leader who must be dedicated to better understanding and appreciating the interrelationship of the school-based budgeting and academic planning processes.

While many school leaders are focused on obtaining more money for their schools in an era of increased mandates and state funding constraints, other school administrators are concentrating on a much more timely and relevant question: Are schools allocating, budgeting, and spending their money intelligently (Park, 2004)? A recent review by the National Conference of State Legislatures (2003b) reveals that states still face a total budget gap of $2.8 billion. While this figure sends chills up and down the spines of school officials across the nation, this truth does not belie the fact that 31 states have made across-the-board spending cuts, and 11 of these states have made targeted cuts to K–12 education (National Conference of State Legislatures, 2003a). Therefore, school budgeting, unlike the finance side of educational funding, is directly related to the allocation of those specified, and far too often, scarce sources of funding dollars at the school level. To coin a financial term, the "bottom-line" to adequately and effectively delineating between school finance and school budgeting can be summed up by one simple word, *allocation.* Allocation is the key to understanding the school budgeting process. Allocation, as well as appropriate and efficient funding, is not only important to state public education systems, the amount of money schools receive for budgetary purposes is critical to continued student success and achievement (Thompson & Wood, 2001). Nevertheless, school leaders must realize and understand that the school budgeting process is much more than the technical skill associated with the term *allocation*. Exceptional school leaders recognize that effective budgeting must be an integrated approach that incorporates team planning, visionary leadership, and data analysis to establish instructional priorities for necessary funding. These integrated approaches to school budgeting are explored in more depth in Chapters 4 and 5.

Sources of School Funding

The key to understanding sources of school funding is to realize that the expenditures correlated with student educational needs are affected by whether federal, state, and local governments appropriately share in the responsibility for supporting our schools (Thompson, et al., 1994). Naturally, adequate and equitable funding has become a critical issue not only with educators but with politicians and taxpayers as well. The reason why appropriate, adequate, and equitable funding has become a contested issue in public education is related to the fact that our founding fathers failed to provide any arrangements for education in the federal constitution. As a result, the funding of schools has become the responsibility of individual states, whether by design or by default, and in most instances not by choice. By placing the responsibility for public education funding in the hands of individual states, our nation has become, in reality, 51 systems of education and, more notably, 51 sources of school funding (Swanson & King, 1997).

Education is the largest single budgetary component of state and local governments (National Center for Education Statistics, 2005a). School districts receive nearly all of their funding for instruction, either directly or indirectly, from federal, state, and local governments; although the majority of this funding comes from local and state revenues as revealed in Table 1.2. While school districts depend, and most certainly place special emphasis, on the amount of federal funds received, the percentage of federal support for schools is relatively insignificant in relation to state and local funding. For example, many states provide well over 50% of school district funding. As also noted in Table 1.2, federal funding typically amounts to less than 10–15% of a district's funding dollars, with local revenue coming close to or exceeding that of the state funding allotments (National Center for Education Statistics, 2005a).

Table 1.2   Percentage of Revenues by State for Education

State	Local Revenue	State Revenue	Federal Revenue
US	42.80	48.70	8.50
AL	30.90	57.60	11.60
AK	25.50	56.80	17.70
AR	33.00	55.20	11.70
AZ	40.20	48.40	11.40
CA	31.30	58.90	9.90
CO	50.40	43.10	6.50
CT	57.40	37.40	5.20
DE	28.00	63.40	8.60
DC	86.20	0.00	13.80
FL	45.80	43.60	10.50
GA	43.70	48.20	8.10
HI	1.70	90.10	8.20
ID	31.10	59.10	9.80
IL	58.50	33.00	8.50
IN	33.50	58.80	7.60
IA	46.00	46.60	7.40
KS	33.80	57.10	9.10
KY	30.70	58.80	10.60
LA	37.70	49.10	13.20
MA	48.10	42.90	8.90
MD	55.00	38.30	6.70
ME	53.10	40.90	6.00
MI	28.90	63.30	7.80
MN	20.20	73.80	5.90
MO	56.20	35.80	8.00
MS	30.80	53.80	15.40
MT	39.20	46.30	14.50
NE	56.70	34.40	8.90
NH	45.80	48.90	5.20
NJ	52.20	43.50	4.30
NM	12.90	72.10	15.00
NV	62.80	30.20	7.00
NC	26.70	63.70	9.60
ND	47.90	36.80	15.30
NY	47.50	45.60	7.00
OH	48.70	44.80	6.40
OK	32.60	54.70	12.70
OR	40.00	50.90	9.10
PA	55.60	36.60	7.70
RI	51.50	42.00	6.50

(Continued)

Table 1.2 (Continued)

State	Local Revenue	State Revenue	Federal Revenue
SC	42.10	48.10	9.80
SD	50.60	33.70	15.70
TN	46.10	43.80	10.00
TX	49.20	40.90	9.90
UT	34.30	56.40	9.30
VA	53.80	39.60	6.60
VT	25.30	67.80	7.00
WA	29.20	61.80	9.00
WI	40.60	53.40	6.10
WV	27.90	61.40	10.60
WY	40.30	50.90	8.80

SOURCE: Data was collected from the National Center for Education Statistics [Online]. Retrieved June 16, 2005, from http://nces.ed.gov

NOTE: The totals for each row may not equal 100% due to rounding or due to states receiving intermediate revenue for education. Intermediate revenue is defined as receipts from county or regional governments that are typically quite small or nonexistent in most states.

Naturally, a prerequisite for understanding the budgetary process is a keen realization of where the money comes from—the sources of money received to operate school districts. In financial circles, the appropriate terms are *revenue, income,* and *fiduciary* funding (Bannock, et al., 1998). The opposite side of the "money received" coin is *expenditure,* or "money spent." We will examine sources of income in more detail later in this chapter. However, to better understand the relationship between revenue and expenditure, Figure 1.1 reveals, on a per-pupil basis, the revenue and expenditures of Texas schools during the fiscal year, 2003–2004. The revenue amounts displayed in Figure 1.1 combine state aid and property tax levy figures from state agencies with the amounts in the budget for other sources of school revenue.

Revenue is obtained primarily from tax collection and the sale of bonds. The tax collection funds provide the basis, in fact the majority, of money received and money expended for the instructional and operational aspects of a school district. Bond sales provide revenue necessary for the construction of new school facilities.

Income is a particular funding category that is representative of funds received from the sale of goods and services. A perfect example of income funding is the district food services program. Since income can be generated from the sale of food items in the school cafeteria, district

Figure 1.1   Revenue and Expenditures per-Pupil, Texas School Budgets,
                  2003–2004

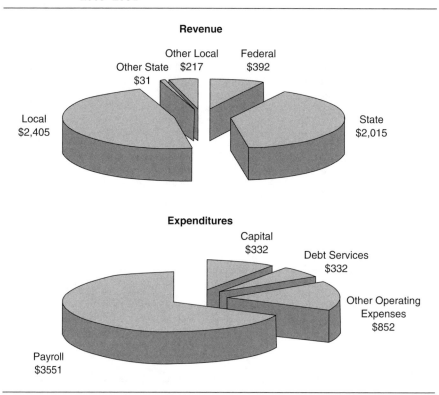

Revenue

Other State $31
Other Local $217
Federal $392
Local $2,405
State $2,015

Expenditures

Capital $332
Debt Services $332
Other Operating Expenses $852
Payroll $3551

SOURCE: Figures utilized in this report were provided by the Property Tax Division
of the Texas Comptroller's Office and the Texas Education Agency (2004).

administrators must develop budgets that project sales and anticipate
expenditures, and then they must implement and monitor a budget.
While a food services program or a food services director may at times
be an irritant to a school administrator, both are essentially important
because of the potential for additional school district income.

The fiduciary category refers to funds that are received from dona-
tions and thus must be managed by or entrusted to a school district in
the most legal and ethical manner possible. While these dollars are
important, such funds are generally not critical to the instructional
operation of a school district. However, these same dollars may be
very significant to a school that needs additional dollars to finance
school-related initiatives and activities not normally funded by a
school district. A perfect example of fiduciary receipts are monies generated from fundraisers and collected by student clubs, campus organizations, graduating classes, or booster clubs; as a result, the school
district must agree to be the depository of these funds and must ensure
that the funds are expended appropriately (Vail, 1999).

Expenditures are exactly that—money spent. Whenever money is spent, the expenditure must be charged against a revenue account and source. School leaders will invariably note that within their budget software listings or on their budget spreadsheets the accounting term *encumbered* appears. Encumbered or encumbrance, by definition, is by no means the same as expenditure. However, both terms maintain a compelling correlation in terms of the budgetary process. For example, when a specified school account is used to initiate a purchase order, the funds are immediately set aside or encumbered, indicating that the dollars for products or services ordered have been committed. At this point, a school leader can expect the purchase order to be processed, and when the goods are received, a payment will be submitted. When the payment has been issued, an expenditure of district dollars has occurred.

The expenditure of funds must always be accounted for, and thus as a school leader, you may complain from time to time about the numerous business department forms that have to be completed, such as purchase orders, requisitions, travel reimbursements, and vouchers, all of which are examples of the paperwork commonly associated with district expenditures. Filling out these forms may seem to be a nuisance, but they ensure fiscal accountability, and each may very well be the necessary documentation to keep you, the school leader, out of a legal entanglement (Kemerer & Walsh, 2005). Mutter and Parker (2004) in their book, *School Money Matters: A Handbook for Principals,* note that financial forms and accompanying safeguards are "designed to meet three important school financial objectives: (1) to protect school staff from suspicion of theft or laxness, (2) to protect school assets, and (3) to fulfill the stewardship responsibility for public funds expected by the general public" (p. 1). When fiscal accountability is ignored, for whatever reason, the end result is less than attractive—much less. For example, consider the following "no way out" situation involving an accounting clerk.

Veronica's Problem

Veronica, an accounting clerk, was often embarrassed and angered by the numerous telephone calls she received at work from creditors who were demanding money for her husband's excessive expenditures. These accumulated debts arose from her husband's business. Veronica was just as responsible as her husband for these extensive debts, since she and her husband resided in a community property state. His debts were her debts. Their financial predicament had reached a level of desperation, and Veronica knew something had to be done.

One day at work, Veronica was seen slipping a vendor check into her purse by a friend and colleague, Jenny. Jenny had a moral and ethical obligation to report the fraudulent actions of Veronica. However, Jenny was reluctant to do so because her identity as a "whistleblower" might be revealed. Some months later, a company-hired Certified Public Accountant (CPA) took basic steps to prevent organizational fraud. He soon learned from Jenny of the embezzlement scheme that Veronica was regularly playing out at the office.

Veronica subsequently confessed that she was processing certain invoices twice. When she was in need of cash, Veronica would make a copy of the invoice before stamping the original. The two were almost indistinguishable. Next, she would process the original invoice, send it on for approval, and then process the "copied" invoice several days later. The same invoice was paid twice. When the vendor realized the overpayment, it would send a refund check that always landed on Veronica's desk. Veronica pocketed the check and, in turn, her husband forged an endorsement and subsequently deposited the check in his business account. The whole fraudulent scheme occurred over a two-year period, and more than $200,000 was embezzled. Veronica was ultimately indicted and convicted (Wells, 2002).

Veronica's problem is an obvious example of how school-based budgeting is much more than a technical or managerial skill and process. One must understand that the budgeting process constantly overlaps into the arena of certain behaviors—visionary, integrity, fairness, and ethical, for example. These behavioral concepts, along with their impact on school-based budgeting, will be explored in more detail in Chapter 2.

Finally, district revenue funds are generated by and large through taxes assessed on the general public and on for-profit businesses. As was noted earlier in this chapter, school districts receive the vast majority of their revenue for instruction from federal, state, and local governments. Let's now examine specific sources of generated revenue or income for school districts.

Federal Sources of Income

Federal revenue comes in the form of different and distinct sources of transfer payments known as *general, categorical,* and *block grants* aid. General and categorical aid, the major source of federal income for education, has significantly impacted and expanded the capabilities of school districts to enhance student achievement (Swanson & King, 1997).

General aid flows from federal and state governments with few limitations to local school districts. General aid provides the largest proportion of financial support for school operations. Local school boards and district administrators largely determine how such income will be allocated to educational programs and other related expenditures.

Categorical aid is a source of funding to school districts that links funding to specific objectives of the government in support of specified programs such as special education, gifted and talented education, career and technology education (formerly vocational education), and compensatory education. Unlike general aid, categorical aid must be utilized for certain groups of students (e.g., those with disabilities), a specific purpose (e.g., pupil transportation), or a particular project (e.g., construction of a school facility). Most often, categorical aid calls for annual applications, documentation of expenditures, and frequent program evaluations and audits. Categorical aid was once the predominant form of federal income to states and school districts. However, other forms of federal aid now serve as income supplements with fewer restrictions at the local level. In recent years, much of the categorical aid has been absorbed into block grants to reduce the local paperwork and personnel productivity burdens associated with federal funds to education (Swanson & King, 1997).

Block grants aid provides funding for a wide range of services, with federal requirements for planning, implementing, and assessing programs being much less stringent than those associated with categorical aid. Block grants provide for local funding on the number of students rather than through a competitive application process that identifies particular educational needs. Block grants provide local districts greater latitude and further give district administrators more discretion in program designs. As a result, local school boards and district administrators typically prefer block grants because they minimize governmental scrutiny and control, and they further provide for more opportunities for district officials to meet local priorities (Brewer, et al., 2001).

The largest of the block grant programs is Title I funding which reaches 11 million disadvantaged students. Title I monies, in the form of block grants, go directly to school districts and schools where it is most needed and fund, for example, extra teachers and programs such as *Success for All*—all of which help students master reading, writing, and mathematics (Feldman, 2000). Over the years, block grant funding has served to focus on and improve proven programs that have turned around entire schools and even school districts.

A perfect example is the educational system in Hartford, Connecticut, where student achievement in this poor, urban school district—once ranked academically lowest in the state—recently made significant improvements in the area of math and reading test scores (Congressional Quarterly, 2000).

Federal aid has certainly served to promote equity and equality in education over the last 25–30 years and has generally improved the quality of education for all students. However, the "strings attached" or restrictions and regulations that generally accompany such financial aid have often been considered nothing more than unwarranted intervention by the "feds" into affairs at the local level. As opposed to promoting efficiency in funding, the federal dollars, and attached stipulations, have often stifled local school officials' efforts in addressing student needs and community considerations for better schools (Swanson & King, 1997).

State Sources of Income

Most states have as their source of income property taxes, sales taxes, and income taxes. These sources of income determine the amount of state funding for school districts. This revenue allotment is then typically distributed to the differing school districts across a state by means of a *state-aid formula* (Jones, 1985). These funding formulas are generally driven by student enrollment, and again this aid comes primarily from assessed taxes. While property taxation remains the major source of local revenue for schools, the local tax base is typically insufficient to support a school district. Therefore, most states have developed state-aid formulas as the basis for infusing some fundamental element of equity from district to district within a state. State-aid formulas are the result of legislative choice and litigation force (Fisher, et al., 1999).

The purpose of state aid formulas is to counterbalance disparities in educational equity and opportunity that would most certainly be present if school districts depended solely on the local tax base (Guthrie, et al., 1988). An example of such a disparity is illustrated in the following scenario: A school district located along a state coastline near a major seaport is the recipient of tax dollars generated by several major petrochemical corporations. These taxable entities generate significant per-pupil wealth on the basis of taxable property. A second school district, similar in size and population but located further inland, is solely dependent on the agribusiness industry, and thus the district receives only limited revenue from its economically depressed tax base. Another example is often evident in states with large urban centers which face vast disparities in their tax base due to ever-growing suburbs and the related citizenry and corporation flight to the nearby bedroom communities.

Most states develop foundation programs to facilitate the state-aid formulas. These programs are the mechanism by which the equalization of resources from district to district can occur. The foundation programs allow for the difference in the cost of a school program and the amount each school district must contribute from local taxation (Thompson & Wood, 2001). Today, very complex state-aid formulas advance the foundation programs, and such formulas are generally related to a fictitious "weighted student" consideration. After the foundation program cost is determined by formula, financing is equalized by determining the local share for each individual district and then the remainder is funded by state aid. State aid for individual school districts equal the foundation program cost minus the local share. However, it is worth noting that state aid formulas have come under intense scrutiny in recent years, and to date, legal challenges related to formula funding continue to come before the United States Supreme Court (Garner, 2004). For example, the issue of equity in relation to educational opportunities for all students regardless of socioeconomic background and/or ethnicity continues to be a critical issue before the courts, both state and federal, as well as state legislatures. Inequities have long plagued public schools, particularly in the area of financing educational facilities with minimal funding reforms and state-led efforts. This is not to say that the courts have completely ignored equity in public school financing. Consideration by the courts is most certainly revealed in several recent court cases in which lawsuits have demanded that states provide adequate and equitable educational facilities. Unfortunately, the operative term and process utilized in response to these legal entanglements has most often been nothing more than "adequate." Court cases from Texas (*Edgewood v. Kirby*, 1986 and *West Orange Cove CISD v. Neeley*, 2005), Ohio (*DeRolph* v. *State of Ohio*, 2000), New Mexico (*Alamogordo* vs. *Morgan*, 1995), West Virginia (*Pauley* v. *Bailey*, 1994), and Tennessee (*Small Schools*, 1988) serve to exemplify just a few decisions that have impacted, often minimally, equitable facilities and funding for all students (Brimley & Garfield, 2005).

Local Sources of Income

The majority of school districts in the United States obtain their locally generated income from at least one of the following sources: *ad valorem* (property) taxes, sales taxes, income taxes, or *sumptuary* (sin) taxes.

Property tax is the most common source of income for school districts. Typically, a tax is levied on property such as land and buildings that are owned by individuals and businesses. Generally, a property tax is determined on the basis of a percentage of the true market value of each piece of property assessed. These assessments are rarely accurate since local assessors either over- or under-assess the value of the property. Typically, the assessed value of the property is adjusted to an agreed-upon percentage of the market value when it is sold (Funkhouser, 1999).

Property taxation remains a largely complicated and particularly controversial source of local income for school districts because numerous complexities are associated with the assessment process. Homestead exemptions, tax abatements, legal entanglements, taxpayer associations, and under-assessments of property all serve to erode the "true" tax base for individual school districts. However, property taxation continues to be the most stable income base as well as a dependable source of income for school districts (Hylbert, 2002).

Another form of taxation that serves as a revenue source for many school districts is the sales tax which is quite popular in many states. This tax is assessed on the price of a good or service when it is purchased by a consumer. The seller of the merchandise or service collects the sales tax dollars, which is included in the purchase price, and transfers the amount of the sales tax to the state comptroller offices. Since this tax is based on sales, its yield is quite elastic. As a result, a sales tax as a form of revenue for school districts is only as stable as the economy (Garner, 2004).

Some school districts acquire their local source of income from a state income tax that is levied on corporations and/or individuals. Income taxation is the most widely accepted form of taxation for schools, and it is considered the most equitable of any source of taxation. Over the years, states have initiated income taxation as a source of funding education. In a majority of our nation's states, the taxing of income is considered the most appropriate mechanism for property tax relief. In addition, income taxation provides a high revenue yield and creates minimal social and economic disruption (Swanson & King, 1997).

Very few school districts derive income from sumptuary taxes on items such as tobacco, alcohol, and gambling. This type of taxation is somewhat different than the income and property tax because it is based on "sin" sales. Due to this dependency, the tax yield is quite elastic and thus, it—much like a sales tax—is only as stable as the economy. Also, the tobacco and alcohol industries extensively lobby state legislators, and, as a result, this type of taxation has not necessarily served as a viable taxing alternative (Guthrie, et al., 1988).

Another source of educational revenue can be dollars received from a lottery—an assessment on legalized gambling. Many individuals believe that the proceeds from a state lottery system provide great sums of income for education. Nothing is further from the truth, although this argument has been used for years by proponents for the legalization of state lotteries. Research reveals that the individuals most susceptible to the promises of a lottery are those in the lower income bracket, which further makes the proceeds from this form of state income quite regressive (Birrup, et al., 1999). Most notably, there is no evidence that any state lottery has significantly supported or benefited any school district or, for that matter, public education in general (Jones & Amalfitano, 1994).

Now that we have explored several of the possible sources of income for school districts, it becomes apparent that wherever the funding is derived, allocations to individual schools at the district level are made, and thus school leaders have as one of their many responsibilities the task of developing a budget. Developing a school budget can be an arduous undertaking but it can be completed with some sense of ease and satisfaction when a school leader is able to utilize specific steps or methods to effectively and efficiently plan for a successful school budget.

Ten Steps to Budgeting Success

There are ten important steps to successful and effective budgeting. These steps are identified below with brief descriptors explaining why each of them is critical to a school leader's success in developing, implementing, and evaluating a budget.

1. Determine the Allotment

Before deciding what educationally related expenditures to make, it is important to know the specified funding allotment that has been appropriated within each budgetary category. Furthermore, certain budgetary allotments can only be used for a variety of specified services and expenditures at the school level. As a result, some funds are more restrictive than others. These restricted funds are often associated with Title I, Bilingual Education, and Special Education dollars and programs. Restricted funds are examined in more detail in Chapter 6.

2. Identify Fixed Expenditures

Recognize and note those expenditures that do not vary from year to year. Set aside the necessary funds in the amount of the fixed expenditures before building the school budget.

3. Involve All Parties

Whether at school or home, or within any organization, everyone should be involved in the budgetary decision-making process. By involving as many parties as possible, a school leader can more effectively ensure ultimate "buy-in" as related to the school budget. All parties include, for example, faculty and staff, parents, students, community members, and any other interested individuals. When all parties are provided with the opportunity for input, with their particular issues being given noteworthy consideration, "buy-in" is more likely, and any plans, preparations, or budgetary considerations are less susceptible to interference or possible sabotage by a disgruntled member of the learning community.

4. Identify Potential Expenditures

The effective school leader reviews past budgetary records to better identify and predict future expenditures. By knowing which expenditures are necessary and imperative, a school administrator can help faculty and staff avoid making impulsive purchases.

5. Cut Back

Most newly created school budgets are over-budgeted. As a school leader, it is your responsibility to examine all potential expenditures and determine where cutbacks can occur. Remember that cutting back too severely can build discontent among the faculty. School budgets that are continually out of balance lead to greater fiscal sacrifices and may very well lead to a financial point of no return. So cut back as necessary and be aware that budgeting is an exercise in self-discipline for all parties. A simple yet effective way to cut back involves implementing a thorough physical inventory. School administrators should do more than just go through the motions when completing a physical inventory. Such an inventory can very well identify areas where unnecessary purchases can be avoided. Consider the following: Why continue to purchase supplies such as chalk, erasers, staples, paperclips, etc. when said or similar items may very well be in abundance in a classroom or office closet or central warehouse?

While cutting back is important in the school business, the creative school administrator is always seeking "windfalls." Additional funding sources are available to those administrators who are willing to put forth the time and effort to seek financial assistance. For example, one school in a property-poor district utilized the campus leaders, site-based team members, and the parent-teacher organization to canvas the community seeking adopt-a-school partners. A partnership with a large retail corporation proved extremely successful. The school was able to acquire not only essential supplies and merchandise for student use and consumption, the corporation also provided funding for computers and other important resources that otherwise would not have been available to either students or staff. Therefore, instead of living by the adage *Show me the money,* adopt a more useful motto: *I'll find the money!* An excellent source for finding, raising, and attracting extra dollars for a school or school system is *Fiscal Fitness for School Administrators* by Robert D. Ramsey (2001).

6. Avoid Continued Debts

The effective budget manager knows exactly what funds are out of balance and where debt is or has accumulated. Many school leaders fail to list and total their debts during the course of the fiscal year, and thus wait until the end of the school year to make necessary budget revisions to amend for such shortsighted calculations. In addition, some states and school districts do not allow individual school-sites to acquire debts on a monthly or annual basis. Such a policy is not only worthwhile, but wise. Nevertheless, debt reduction can be readily achieved by avoiding unnecessary purchases. Consider the following example: Recall the wise, old advice that was shared with you and your spouse when first married: "Most unhappiness is caused by giving up what you want most for what you want at the moment!" Life as a school leader is stressful enough without further complicating matters by overspending at the expense of the school budget, if not the student population. Remember, the most important word you can learn to use as a school administrator, specifically in connection with the school budget, may very well be *no*—especially when it comes to unwise or inappropriate spending!

7. Develop a Plan

Any budget—school, home, or business—should be based on a plan. From a school perspective, an educationally centered action or improvement plan has to be developed to target and prioritize instructional goals and objectives along with school programs and activities. In addition, a second plan of action (school budget plan) is designed to identify budgetary priorities, focusing on appropriations and expenditures. Furthermore, such a plan is designed to determine what programs and activities match the budgetary allotments for the school.

8. Set Goals

Many would insist that "setting goals" should be first and foremost on any list of budgetary considerations. No argument here. However, it is important that the effective school leader do all the preliminary work of determining what funds are available before determining how to spend the funds. Nevertheless, setting goals (whether management or instructional) is the one fundamental step that all self-disciplined administrators utilize and the one step that most are—unfortunately—inclined to skip. As the budgetary process is developed and established, it is imperative that consideration be given to those issues, demands, and dictates, simply put: those purchases that are valued as necessities or non-negotiables. Again, by involving all parties, goals can be identified and set. But remember, setting goals takes more than money; it takes time, effort, determination, and considerable thought and preparation. How does a school leader, working in conjunction with a learning community, set goals? Listed below are a few essential considerations.

1. Establish priorities—ascertain what is instructionally important.

2. Decide what can wait until later in the budget cycle or until the next school year.

3. Assess what is important today but will not be tomorrow.

4. Determine what priorities are meaningful compared to those that are mandated.

5. Submit various proposed budgets (by department, grade level, etc.) to the site-based committee which serves in part to determine if the allocated dollars within each budget correlate with the established goals of the school.

Finally, remember that goals can and will change. Therefore, as the school leader and budget manager, it is imperative that you, in collaboration with the school's decision-making team, regularly assess and evaluate each budgetary goal and make any necessary changes as the school year progresses.

9. Evaluate the Budget

After a plan has been developed, it needs to be put into action. Take time; meet at least once a month with the decision-making team to evaluate the budget process to better determine if the established goals and the budgeted dollars are equitable and compatible. Planned budgeting and goal evaluation go hand-in-hand. Always seek answers to the following questions:

1. Is the budget within the allotted limits, or do adjustments (amendments) need to be made on the basis of alternative need or changing vision?

2. Is progress being made toward the established goals?

3. Are purchases coinciding with planned goals?

4. Has the budget process been successful when compared with the established plan and goals?

5. What improvements can be made in the future?

10. Abide by the Budget

Abiding by the budget means living by the budget. As the school leader, you must set the example in all areas of instructional leadership for others at your school to follow. This is most certainly true in relation to the school budget. "Time on task" is an old adage in our business, but nothing rings more true in terms of the school budget and the necessity for you—the instructional leader—to monitor, evaluate, and abide by the budget and the accompanying action plan that you have developed.

Final Thoughts

As the school leader, you should invest the necessary time and energy to deal with the funds appropriated to you and the learning community. Wise budgeting can bring you and your students a sense of accomplishment and even fulfillment—most notably when the instructional program improves and student achievement excels. However, before you budget, plan. Planning means developing a vision, establishing goals, determining objectives, and initiating strategies for school implementation in a continuing effort to increase student achievement. Each of these planning indicators is an essential element in the development of an effective budget using an integrated approach to budgeting.

A budget is not a "once-a-year" event, something you establish and never examine again. A budget must be abided by and it must be reviewed and amended on a regular basis as the needs of its academic counterpart change. This requires ongoing evaluation and revision. Nothing in life is perfect, and the same holds true for school budgets. Academic goals—while imperative to the budgeting process—have to be reorganized and adjusted from time to time. Action planning and goal development, academic improvement, and budget management must be integrated if school leaders intend to bring about educational excellence and increased student achievement. Certain standards that will be analyzed in Chapter 2 must be emphasized and incorporated by the school leader if the budgeting process is going to meet with success. Abide by the budget; make the necessary changes, and always follow-up with on-going evaluation. Allow self-discipline to be the guiding factor in budgetary decision-making, and remember that an integrated budget and academic action plan will not work unless you do!

Discussion Questions

1. Consider each of the local sources of income that support school districts. What are the advantages and disadvantages of each in relation to equity, yield, and taxpayer acceptance?

2. Why is it important to integrate the school budget and the academic or action plan? How can the budget and academic planning processes be integrated?

3. Which of the budgeting myths pose a more fundamental obstacle to the school administrator in relation to the development of a campus budget? Why?

4. What might be considered a serious risk factor that a school administrator could face in relation to fiduciary receipts?

5. What are the commonalities and differences of the three federal sources of district income?

6. Should any one of the 10 steps to budgeting success be considered more important than the others? Which one and why?

7. To better understand the percentage of revenues, as exemplified in Figure 1.1, contact the official state education Web site as well as the school business administrator or superintendent of schools to determine the sources of income for the school district.

Case Study Application: Fiscal Issues and the New Principal

The application of a case study as related to campus visioning, planning, and budgeting will be presented at the conclusion of each chapter in this book to provide applicable and relevant workplace scenarios so the reader can put into practice the knowledge acquired through textual readings.

Part I—"Boy, Do I Have a Lot to Learn!"

Dr. Ryan Paulson, new principal at Mountain View Middle School, had arrived at Vista Ridge Independent School District from a neighboring state. While Dr. Paulson certainly knew and understood certain aspects of the fiscal and budgetary processes of his former state, he realized that he needed a refresher course in budgeting, especially as related to the fiscal issues he might face in his new state and school district.

Dr. Paulson decided to stop by the administrative offices of Vista Ridge Independent School District and visit with the superintendent, Dr. Mildred Dunn, as well as the associate superintendent for school finance, Dr. Gene Corley. Certainly, these two individuals could bring him "up to speed" on the fiscal expectations of his new state and school district. As good fortune would have it, the first two individuals he encountered, as he stepped into the main offices, were Dr. Dunn and Dr. Corley. Dr. Corley, a most gregarious individual, was the first to see the new principal and hollered out at him: "Hey, hot-shot, did you get to eat some of that good barbeque that I told you about?" Dr. Paulson responded that he had not yet had the opportunity, but he was looking forward to getting over to Elginton for a tasty plate of sausage and ribs. Dr. Dunn then spoke up and asked what was on the young man's mind? "Well, since you've inquired" replied Dr. Paulson, "I need some guidance about the state's fiscal policies and the district's budgeting practices." Dr. Dunn suggested that all three step into Dr. Corley's office for, as she put it, "a quick review of School Budgeting 101."

"School budgeting and finance, in this era of change, is a real juggling act," noted Dr. Dunn. "However, let's start with the basics and get you on the right track before school starts," suggested the superintendent. Thus began an afternoon of one learning experience after another. By the conclusion of the meeting, Dr. Paulson had come to realize that a costly war on terror, an economy hit hard by high energy costs, and federal and state accountability standards and mandates, as well as numerous other conditions had negatively influenced the ability of both the state and local districts to raise tax revenues to meet the demands of educating today's students. These challenges most notably and negatively reflected on each school's list of priorities and each district's ability to finance them.

The bottom line of the first meeting between the three parties revolved around the realization that education must be viewed as an investment in human capital. Resource allocations to public schools are the responsibility not only of the federal and state governments but of the local school district as well. Moreover, funding the rapidly increasing costs of education is an ongoing challenge for schools, and such funding is becoming more frequently associated with accountability expectations and standards at the local level.

A most interesting point that had been made by Dr. Dunn related to the proposition that educational services and funding must be provided with equality, but could it be provided equitably? "Wow" thought Dr. Paulson to himself, "Does anyone have an answer to that question?" Furthermore, Dr. Paulson recognized that even though the cost of education continues to increase annually, this burden is eased when one realizes that while the costs of public schooling involves money, mostly in salaries, much of the cost is readily returned to the marketplace, thus benefiting the economy, consumers, local households, individual citizens, and most important, local students. This meeting reminded Dr. Paulson of a statement of fact that had been drilled into his head by a former professor in his principal certification program at Union State University: "While the cost of education may be high, the defining and measuring result must always be quality in learning."

Finally, Dr. Paulson had been directed to the state's Web site regarding Operating Accounting Codes and Structures. It was essential that he quickly learn the proper budgetary coding procedures as dictated by the state's education agency. He had already memorized the Web site address, and was now ready to adapt to the new coding structure and fiscal practices associated with his new school budget. As he left the district's administrative offices he could not help but think: "Boy, do I have a lot to learn!"

Application Questions

1. What is meant by the following terms: *adequacy, equality, equitable, human capital, quality?*

2. How is the theoretical concept, "education must be viewed as an investment in human capital," realized in your community? Provide concrete examples.

3. Can educational services and funding be provided with equality and equity? Support your answer.

4. What is meant by the quote: "While the cost of education may be high, the defining and measuring result must always be quality in learning?" How does this proposition relate to the concept of vision development?

5. Contact your business department administrator or school superintendent or state finance person to obtain a copy of the state's Operating Accounting Code structure. How is this structure similar to or different from the example utilized in Chapter 1?

Part II—"Well, It's My Money!"

Dr. Ryan Paulson, now into his second semester as principal at Mountain View Middle School, had just developed—in collaboration with his site-based decision-making team—the campus budget for the next school year. He had learned so much since that initial meeting with Dr. Dunn and Dr. Corley the preceding July, but, as is always the case, so much more was yet to be realized. The budget for Mountain View Middle School included funds to retain three special education aides who assisted with the inclusion program that was adopted last school year after significant research by and professional development for faculty and staff. These aides worked with special needs students who warranted considerable assistance and who required significant class time to complete the assigned academic tasks.

When the budget was submitted to the associate superintendent for secondary instruction for approval, she cut the aide positions and transferred the funds to the appropriate account for purchasing laptop computers for the recently renovated middle school computer lab. Although Dr. Paulson realized the importance of purchasing the computers and had thought that the school district would fund such items, he believed that the functioning of the special needs students in the inclusion program would suffer by the budgetary reduction of the three special education aide positions. Anyway, he thought to himself: "Well, it's my money and I should be able to spend it how I please!"

Application Questions

1. Regarding his concerns about the transfer of funds as made by the Associate Superintendent of Secondary Instruction, how should Dr. Paulson address this budgetary issue and decision-making consideration? How is this particular issue related to a trio of concepts: integrity, fairness, and ethics?

2. What are the potential implications as related to the decision made by the associate superintendent in relation to the site-based decision-making team, the school community?

3. Identify the possible repercussions as related to the special education department. What legal issues must be considered as related to the removal of the special education paraprofessionals, as well as the maintenance of services to the students, in light of Individual Education Plans (IEPs) and associated stipulations? Can funds that were

originally designated for the special education paraprofessional be transferred and used to purchase computers? If such action is legal, is it fair or ethical? Support your conclusions.

4. Immediately after the budget changes are made public, Dr. Paulson receives several telephone calls from the parents of a number of the students in the inclusion program. These parents are disturbed about the effects on the learning environment in their children's classes as a result of the loss of the aides. How can Dr. Paulson best respond to these parents?

5. What did Dr. Paulson infer by stating: "Well, it's my money and I should be able to spend it how I please"? Could such a statement be justified in relation to the Ten Steps to Budgeting Success? If so, support your answer.

2

The Budget-Vision Relationship and the National Standards

You do not lead by hitting people over the head—that's assault, not leadership.

—Dwight David Eisenhower

School leaders are faced with the challenge of improving student academic achievement in a time of contracting resources and in the face of a host of other challenges such as:

- Enrollment in public schools is at an all-time high of 53 million. It will continue to rise due to birth rates and immigration.
- There is a shortage of teachers. The U.S. Department of Education projects that 2.2 million new teachers will be needed over the next 10 years.

- Many communities face a critical shortage of citizens who are willing to serve on school boards.
- Fewer educators with leadership potential are willing to serve as principals.
- More than $112 billion is needed to repair, replace, or modernize public schools.
- The dropout rate is 13% for black students, 25% for Hispanic students, and 8% for white students. (AASA, 1999)

Innovative and courageous leadership combined with fresh ideas will enable us to conquer these and other challenges in our schools.

School budgeting. School vision. These are two issues that school leaders must confront on a daily basis. The relationship between school budgeting and vision is as intertwined as is love with marriage. In both cases, you can't have one without the other (Iger, 1998). These two forces, budget and vision, come to us with their own accountability systems. The former is fiscal, the latter is academic. State and federal legislation continue to raise the ante for success in both of these systems by creating new measures that are designed to add increased external accountability for improving student achievement. Among the requirements of the federal No Child Left Behind Act of 2001 are increased accountability for student academic performance, adequate yearly progress, campus and district report cards, and employing and training highly qualified teachers using scientifically based practices (Rebora, 2004; Gonzales, Hamilton & Stetcher, 2003). Technology has given rise to greater and more complicated accounting procedures for both of these systems. Leaders can be overwhelmed as they try to make sense of the sea of data being spewed at them from a variety of sources. With all of the other demands placed on them, what is a school leader to do? We must approach the situation differently.

School budgeting is more than spreadsheets, reports, tracking the expenditure of funds, and the completing of a myriad of accounting forms. It is easy to get caught up in the accounting dimension of budgeting and neglect its companion—vision. It is the integration of vision within the school budgeting process that transforms school budgeting from merely number crunching to purpose-driven expenditures that support academic success for all students. An articulated and shared vision creates the environment that is necessary for planning academic success to flourish for all students.

We must rethink how we approach school budgeting. School budgeting should not simply be an accounting responsibility. As leaders we must leave the primary accounting responsibility to CPAs and the business office. These folks must be allowed to provide the technical expertise and support necessary to meet the regulatory requirements associated with state fiscal accountability standards. Our leadership skills must be used to carry the school budgeting process to the next level. This is achieved by integrating the school vision with the budgeting and academic processes for the purpose of achieving academic success for all students.

Imagine a train heading down a track, as depicted in Figure 2.1. The train is the school. The locomotive represents the school leader. This individual leads the local motivation to create a shared vision for the school. The remaining cars are the school's vision and budget and planning process. The movement of the train down the track is the school year. Like the locomotive, the leader is key to moving the school "down the track." Bringing the cars of vision, budget, and planning are essential, so essential in fact, that they are recognized and supported in the Educational Leadership Constituent Council (ELCC) and Interstate School Leaders Licensure Consortium (ISLLC) standards.

Figure 2.1   The Integrated Budget Train

The school leader is in the locomotive leading the cars of vision, planning, and budgeting. "Yes you can! Yes you can! Yes you can!" comes rolling back from the locomotive for all to hear.

Kathy Myrick, illustrator

The National Educational Leadership Standards

In days gone by, states and professional organizations each had their own standards and proficiencies for school leaders. This lack of a single set of research-based standards led the states and professional organizations to collaborate in developing such standards. The National Policy Board for Educational Administration (NPBEA), a consortium of 10 organizations, emerged with the mission to improve school leadership.

The NPBEA began developing a set of guidelines for advanced programs in educational leadership for the National Council for the Accreditation of Teacher Education (NCATE) (NPBEA, 2001). This action eventually led to the formation of the Educational Leadership Constituent Council that developed the proposed guidelines to be considered by university professors and other groups interested in the formal training of school leaders.

During this same time period, the Council of Chief State School Officers (CCSSO), a national organization of state-level education leaders, created the Interstate School Leaders Licensure Consortium. This consortium was given the task of constructing a framework that would redefine school leadership by creating national educational leadership standards (Murphy & Shipman, 1998; Shipman, Topps & Murphy, 1998).

These efforts to develop national standards, NPBEA through the creation of the ELCC and the CCSSO, were eventually coordinated when the National Policy Board charged the committee working on the ELCC guidelines to incorporate the ISLLC standards in their work (NPBEA, 2001). The result of this action was that the ISLLC standards and the ELCC standards are very similar to each other. This similarity of standards for professional development for practicing school leaders as well as for university preparation programs strengthened the development of educational leaders.

The first six ELCC standards mirror their six ISLLC counterparts. The ELCC, however, added a seventh standard that focuses on the internship experience, which was to be a part of the recommended formal university educational leadership development program. Regardless, the ELCC standards with their program perspective and the ISLLC with their individual perspective were essentially aligned except for the added seventh ELCC standard, and now serve as the benchmark for developing current and future leaders (Council of Chief State School Officers, 1996).

Both the ELCC and ISLLC standards were created with the intent to improve our performance as school leaders, regardless of the title or function of our leadership position. This pair of congruent standards reminds us that improving teaching and learning is a central responsibility of those in leadership positions. The standards require that we be active, not passive, in performing our duties. They also assume that we are collaborative and inclusive in conducting these duties. Finally, the standards do not ascribe to any particular theory of leadership. No one leadership theory has proven to be adequate to be franchised as *the* leadership theory for school administrators. The necessary skills and characteristics of leadership must still be developed and fostered in school leaders (NPBEA, 2002).

Steven Covey (1990) encouraged us in his book, *The Seven Habits of Highly Effective People,* to "begin with the end in mind." In essence, that is exactly what the ELCC and ISLLC standards call on school leaders to do when in each standard we are charged to "promote the success of all students." All means everybody, 100%. Which of us wants our child or grandchild not to meet with academic success? Can we walk down our school's hallways and look at our students and determine which ones we do not want to meet with success? What moral choice do we have but to "promote the success of all students"? This "all students" dimension of the national standards demands a train trip to Utopia for planning big and promoting success. It requires us to revisit our long-time friends—school budgeting and vision—and examine their often-overlooked relationship in the planning process.

Initially we might be criticized for taking this Utopian train trip. Critics will accuse us of not living in the real world. We can suffer through the criticism and cynicism of these sarcastic and skeptic voices because we understand that all children meeting with success is by its very nature a Utopian goal. Visiting Utopia will provide us with a perfect vision for our schools. It is imperative that we begin with a perfect vision for our schools. To begin planning for academic success for all students with a vision that is less than ideal dooms us in our quest for academic success for all children.

Shifts in Knowledge and Skills

Our visit to Utopia begins with an examination of three paradigm shifts identified by Scott Thomas, past executive secretary of the National Policy Board for Educational Administration. In writing an introductory rationale for the ELCC standards, Thomas identifies five broad based shifts in the knowledge and skills required of educational leaders today compared to the traditional knowledge base (NPBEA, 2002). It is significant that the underlying premise of this book—integrating budgeting and vision—is at the center of three of the five shifts identified by Thomas.

From Technical Skills to Interpersonal Skills

This "shift" for school leaders is all about the vision thing. Thomas advances the idea that gaining a common vision for a school involves interpersonal skills rather than technical skills. In order to gain a common vision, principals must generate a learning culture, work with staff in improving instruction, be collaborative, and identify and solve problems, all the while addressing ethnic and gender differences (NPBEA, 2002). As our society has become more pluralistic, we have more groups with greater diversity with which we must work to sculpt a common vision for our schools. Blumberg and Greenfield (1986) note that principals who were effective in advancing a school vision were competent in three skills: (1) articulating a vision for their schools and openly exchanging views with others about its accomplishment; (2) persuading teachers and others in the school community to internalize or incorporate the vision in their daily conduct; and (3) encouraging teachers and others to make personal sacrifices toward its realization. All three of these skills are interpersonal skills.

From Director to Consensus Builder and Motivator

The second broad shift identified by Thomas involves changing from director to consensus builder and motivator. Thompson recognized that involving as many stakeholders in the decision-making process improved the quality of the decision as well as the motivation for ensuring the successful implementation of the decision (NPBEA, 2002). Once again, Blumberg and Greenfield (1992) reinforce these ideas in their research. They found that schools that make meaningful progress toward accomplishing the school vision have principals who (1) are effective in exchanging ideas about the vision with others; (2) regularly encourage sacrifices on behalf of that vision; and (3) work with teachers who freely accept and share the campus vision.

From Resource Allocation to Accountability

Finally, Thomas identifies a broad shift in resource allocation to accountability for learning processes and results. This shift demands that school budgeting, vision, and planning be an integrated process. Thomas asserts that principals can no longer allocate resources that are not tied to measurable objectives. He further professes that the increased emphasis on improving student achievement must focus on accountability (NPBEA, 2002).

We concur with Thomas's broad shifts in knowledge and skills required of today's educational leaders. We advance the proposition that the school budgeting process and the vision process must be integrated and synchronized in order for schools to be successful in improving student academic performance.

An Examination of the ELCC and ISLLC Standards

We propose that while we are in Utopia devising our plan for academic success for all, we give primary consideration to the interrelationship between school budgeting and vision. While neither of these concepts is new, it could be argued that as school leaders we have not given due consideration to the significance of the symbiotic relationship that they have on the academic success of our students and our schools. It is important to consider budgeting and vision simultaneously in the planning process in order to increase our understanding of their influence on each other and the fulfillment of the national standard's clarion call for "academic success for all students." It is imperative that the discussion of school budgeting and vision begin with an examination of each ELCC/ISLLC standard. It is also essential that this examination of the standards be accomplished through a school budgeting and vision lens.

ELCC/ISLLC Standard 1[1]

> A school administrator is an educational leader who promotes the success of all students by facilitating the development, articulation, implementation, and stewardship of a school or district vision of learning that is shared and supported by the school community.

Standard 1, like each of the standards, includes the phrase "success of all students." This phrase requires us to approach budgeting and vision from the premise that we expect all students to meet with success, not just those students who come to school prepared and nurtured by their families, but also those who come to us with little nurturing and minimal preparation. We might do well to stop and re-read the previous statement and allow the significance of it to "sink in." "Success of all students" does not allow us to rationalize or explain away our responsibility to have all students meet with success.

Budgeting, vision, and academic success are intertwined with each other in the planning process. They are not isolated variables operating independently in our school's culture. When we accept this coupling of budgeting and vision and understand their combined effect on academic achievement, then budgeting expands from a fiscal responsibility to a fiscal-vision opportunity that in turn drives our planning for academic success for all students. Regardless of what we think about the provisions or requirements of the No Child Left Behind Act of 2001, its intent is noble in that like the national standards it seeks the Utopian goal of success for all students.

Standard 1 is at the very core of the purpose of this book in that it calls for the melding of vision with budget and planning. Not only must a school leader facilitate the development, articulation, and implementation of a school vision, but the leader must also be a steward of that vision. Stewardship is the administration and management of the financial affairs of another. A school leader ensures that the resources of the school are allocated in a manner that supports the school's vision. The school's budget does not belong to the leader. It belongs to the public who has sacrificed through the payment of taxes to provide the revenues for the budget. We will reserve further conversation on this standard for Chapter 3 where we will examine it in greater detail.

ELCC/ISLLC Standard 2

A school administrator is an educational leader who promotes the success of all students by advocating, nurturing, and sustaining a school culture and instructional program conducive to student learning and staff professional growth.

Standard 2 is a key element in growing the integrated budget-vision-planning process. It is noteworthy that this standard immediately follows Standard 1, which establishes the importance of having a school vision. Once the vision is collaboratively developed, the work is just beginning. As leaders we must advocate, nurture, and sustain a school culture conducive to student learning and staff professional growth. It is the responsibility of the school leader to nurture and develop the school culture (Hoy & Miskel, 2005). This is a responsibility that must not be delegated. It is within the school's culture that the traditions, values, and beliefs of the various stakeholders are manifested (Deal & Peterson, 1990). School leaders must seize the opportunity to define the school's culture. We also must be certain we do not lead with reckless behavior. It is important that we get everyone on board. If we see the importance of an integrated budget planning process and the staff fails to see the need, then the whole process is likely to fail (Daresh, 2001).

What we value as leaders will, through time and labor, be valued in the school's culture. If we value the importance of integrating school vision with the budget and planning process and we advocate and nurture the integrated budget-vision planning process, it will become part of the school's culture. We are likely to hear someone say, "At this school we put our money where our mouth is." As a leader we would translate this comment as an affirmation that: At this school (*at this school*) the stakeholders understand (*we put*) that the budget (*our money*) is aligned with the vision (*where our mouth is*).

Resources must be aligned with the vision of the school during the planning process if the school's culture and instructional program are to be conducive to student learning and staff development. Anything less than aligning the budget with the vision bastardizes the process. This standard will be revisited in greater depth in Chapter 3 and Chapter 5.

ELCC/ISLLC Standard 3

A school administrator is an educational leader who promotes the success of all students by ensuring management of the organization, operations, and resources for a safe, efficient, and effective learning environment.

One attribute of successful school management is the skillful handling of resources—thus the budget connection is established in Standard 3. Resources are not limited to but include both internal and external funding, time, personnel, equipment, and facilities.

Leaders are required to manage resources for a safe, efficient, and effective learning environment. The importance of a safe learning environment to student success is reiterated in the pioneering effective schools research of Ron Edmonds and his colleagues in their effective schools research (Taylor, 2002). The funding dimension of a safe learning environment requires that we properly budget for required safety materials and services.

An efficient learning environment is one that functions well to achieve a desired result without waste. Dollars dedicated to education are difficult to come by. It is imperative that the budgeting process be integrated with the goals and objectives of the campus to obtain optimum results. We cannot afford the luxury of keeping ineffective programs, pet projects, or any other distraction that drains precious resources from the school's plan for implementing its shared vision.

An effective learning environment is one that causes us to achieve our intended goals and objectives. We can have the greatest of intentions and passion but if we have not collaboratively developed our goals and objectives and budgeted our resources to those goals and objectives it is impossible for us to possess an effective learning environment.

ELCC/ISLLC Standard 4

A school administrator is an educational leader who promotes the success of all students by collaborating with families and community members, responding to diverse community interests and needs, and mobilizing community resources.

"Mobilizing community resources," the final phrase in Standard 4, establishes our budget-vision link to this important standard. When school leaders mobilize, they not only organize the fiscal resources, they also organize all stakeholders as they ready them for action to achieve the goals and objectives of their schools.

It is essential that all stakeholders possess ownership of the school's action plan and recognize the importance of allocating community resources to achieve the desired results that are in line with the school's vision. We must remember that the community is literally investing its resources in its children and is expecting a return on the investment in the form of educated, enlightened, and productive individuals. When schools fail to produce this product, the community resources must be reallocated to address our failure in the form of welfare, juvenile detention, and adult prison programs. The failure of our schools to meet the needs of our students creates a domino effect that is felt throughout the community. Failure to meet the school site goals for our students creates a more intensely competitive environment for the community resources as other public institutions vying for the same limited public resources must meet the shortcomings of our school programs.

An example of added costs to the public when education is not successful is found in the prison system. The 1992 National Adult Literacy Survey revealed that 51% of prisoners in state and federal prisons had their high school diploma or equivalent, compared to 76% of the general population. This survey, the most comprehensive assessment of educational backgrounds of prisoners in 20 years, also reported that

11% of inmates reported that they had a learning disability. This is nearly three times the national learning disability rate of 3% (LoBuglio, 2001).

Keeping a person in prison costs more than three times the amount it takes to educate a child. The average per-pupil expenditure for students in U.S. public elementary and secondary schools in 2002–2003 was $8,041. Utah at $4,838 spent the least per-pupil in educating children. New Jersey spent $12,568 per student, making it the largest spender per pupil (NCES, 2005b: Table 5). Dyer (2000) reported that in 1998 the cost for new beds in prisons ranged from $29,311 for a minimum security prison to $70,909 for a maximum security prison and maintaining a prisoner in the bed costs $25,000 per year.

The cost to the public for schools not being successful is also reflected in the median earning of adults based on educational attainment. The more educated a person is, the greater the person's income is likely to be. Conversely, the earlier a person drops out of school, the lower the person's income is likely to be. This relationship between educational attainment and income is shown in Table 2.1 (Colorado Literacy Research Institute, 2001). The cost to our society for students not meeting with academic success is staggering. Assuming a 40-year work career and not adjusting for inflation, the worker with a bachelors degree or higher will earn $ 1,137,680 more in a work career than the student who left the school system with less than a ninth-grade education.

When schools fail to achieve the national standards call for academic success for all students, then schools can expect other systems to compete with them for public resources. It is imperative that students

Table 2.1   Earnings According to Education Attainment

Educational Attainment for Adults Age 25 and Over	Median Earnings 2000
Less than 9th grade	$ 15,241
9th–12th grade, no diploma	$ 17,337
High school graduate	$ 25,264
Some college	$ 27,696
Associate degree	$ 30,773
Bachelors degree or more	$ 43,683

SOURCE: Colorado Literacy Research Initiative.

meet with academic success so that not only do they become greater producers for our society, but the need for other institutions such as prisons and welfare programs is lessened; this, in turn, increases the availability of funds to enrich the services provided by public education.

ELCC/ISLLC Standard 5

A school administrator is an educational leader who promotes the success of all students by acting with integrity, fairness, and in an ethical manner.

Standard 5 reminds us that character does in fact count. We must examine ourselves, our motives, and how we treat others as well as how we carry out our personal and professional missions, and then decide what we are not willing to do in order to achieve our personal and school goals. (See Chapter 7.)

Integrity, fairness, and ethical behavior are a trio of concepts that school leaders struggle to define. Former U.S. Supreme Court Justice Potter Stewart, commenting in the *Jacobellis v. Ohio* case concerning the issue of pornography, stated he could not attempt to define pornography and yet acknowledged, "But I know it when I see it" (Linder, n.d.). Like Stewart, we know what integrity, fairness, and ethical behavior are when we see them, but we struggle to define them.

We could approach this trio of terms utilizing the works of Plato, John Locke, Immanuel Kant, Niccolo Machiavelli, and others, but that might seem detached from the day-to-day challenges we face as school leaders. We depend on our own personal judgment and experiences in determining how we react to given situations. Maybe we should take time from our busy schedules to consider integrity, fairness, and ethical behavior. After all, the "in your face" demands of academic accountability, student discipline, per-pupil expenditure, and a host of other demands provide us with many excuses for bypassing an examination of these terms. Cooper (1998) reminds us that as school leaders we often make administrative decisions using rationality and systematic reflection in a piecemeal fashion. Cooper asserts that we are ad hoc problem solvers, not comprehensive moral philosophers. We only resort to the next level of generality and abstraction when our repertoire of practical moral rules fail to help us reach a decision.

Examining Three Key Terms—The Trio

It is important as we examine Standard 5 in the light of budgeting and vision that we pay close attention to the three key terms found in this standard—integrity, fairness, and ethical manner. (See Table 2.2.)

Table 2.2   Key Terms in ELCC/ISLLC Standard 5

Integrity	Soundness of and adherence to moral principle and character
Fairness	Free from bias, dishonesty, or injustice
Ethics	A system of moral principles

SOURCE: *The Random House Dictionary of the English Language* (Unabridged Edition).

Integrity. Integrity, the first of our trio of ethical terms, is an important dimension of leadership. Leaders who value integrity are not only interested in results but are also interested in relationships. This can be easily illustrated in the world of high-stakes student assessment. Each year, educators are under greater pressure to meet a mandated level of academic performance for their students. The consequences for not achieving these defined goals are increasing. The temptation for school leaders to manipulate these data from a variety of schemes is also increasing.

We must not only consider integrity within the sphere of our academic goals. We must also consider the integrity of our relationships with all of the school's stakeholders. It is essential that we earn the trust of all of the stakeholders if we are to be successful. For integrity to exist we must show genuine concern for others and their personal goals. When concern and integrity exist, trust flourishes and further empowers the leader to lead the school toward its shared vision.

We all know of stories where school leaders succumb to temptation and misrepresent themselves, inappropriately use school funds, or manipulate data. When this is discovered these leaders lose their reputation and effectiveness along with their dignity. It takes a lifetime to build a good reputation and only a minute to lose it. A superintendent from a school of 33,000 students retired from her job with three years remaining on her contract as a result of a controversy associated with recommending a contract to be offered to a firm for the delivery of services to the school district. At issue was her failure to advise the board that she had worked as a consultant for several years for the firm (Borja, 2005). Chapter 5 contains a further examination of the integrity issue from the perspective of a leader's reputation.

High-stakes testing is a prime area for leaders to be tempted to cheat by manipulating data. Variables such as test security, student exemptions, and test preparation become factors. In one school district, eight elementary schools, including a Blue Ribbon campus, were being investigated because of unusual swings in the state test scores (Garza, 2005). In yet another school district, the state math exam scores of 300 sixth-grade students were declared invalid due to cheating by some teachers (Honawar, 2001). Cizek (1999) compiled a list of euphemisms that have been used by educators in attempts to soften the term "cheating." Two of the more creative euphemisms were "falsely reporting success" and "achievement similarities not attributable to chance."

Samuel Johnson said, "Integrity without knowledge is weak and useless, and knowledge without integrity is dangerous and dreadful" (*Columbia*, 1996). Integrity alone will not allow us to meet with success. We must understand every facet of our schools and students. We must have a command of the school's vision and its budget. If we lack integrity, our school is at risk; doubt and fear will replace integrity. People will revert to the selfish nature of man, and the common good of the learning community will be forgotten.

Fairness. Once again, we risk our effectiveness as leaders when we separate the vision from the budget, especially when it comes to fairness. It is essential that we consider both budget and vision as integral parts of the planning process if we are to completely understand the complex nature of fairness.

Fairness, the second of the trio of key terms, does not mean ensuring that everyone gets the same amount of something or the same treatment. Fairness is when everyone receives what is needed in order to successfully accomplish their goals. Some students will need one cup of patience while others will require two, three, or even four cups of patience to reach their goals. Still others will need different resources dedicated to them to ensure their academic success. For example, students with learning disabilities might need greater resources in order to reach their instructional goals than those without disabilities.

When we accept the fact that vision is what drives the budget and that shared vision is designed to help all students achieve their potential, then we begin to understand that fairness requires resources to be allocated on the basis of needs in order to obtain academic goals. Fairness is not dividing the financial pie into equal pieces. For example, Berman and Orion (2003) report that in 2000–01 the Massachusetts per-pupil expenditure for students in special education was $12,416 compared to $6,177 for general education. Medical and social factors impacted the spending difference—not district practices. The financial pie was not divided into equal pieces. Instead, it was apportioned based on meeting the individual needs of students.

Our schools perish when there is a lack of vision. When money is thrown at problems, our selfish nature as humans takes over to be sure we get "our fair share." This usually translates into "get all that I can get." In the absence of an understanding of the budget-vision relationship in the planning process, our greed takes control and the good of the learning community is abandoned.

Unfortunately, fairness does not become a part of a school's social fabric overnight. It cannot be ordered or microwaved into existence. Instead, the leader must keep the budget-vision relationship in front of the team and make in-roads into fairness when opportunities arise. Through persistence, fairness will become valued as part of the school's culture and will manifest itself in ethical behavior.

Ethical Behavior. Ethical behavior is the last of our Standard 5 trio of key terms. Ethical behavior is an essential part of the school leader's persona. Fairness, integrity, and equity are employed as we conduct the school's business. School leaders must act in an ethical manner when handling discipline problems, implementing state mandated accountability testing, managing school budgets, consulting with parents, supervising faculty and staff, and in a host of other situations.

As we continue our examination of the national standards with regard to their implication on budgeting and vision, it is appropriate that we consider the principle of benefit maximization. This principle requires us to make choices that provide the greatest good for the most people. When we are developing our school vision, the process must be one of inclusiveness. Shared vision is about meaningfully involving everyone, not just those with the greatest political clout or the loudest voices in the vision development process. As the school leader we must help craft and share a school vision that not only provides all of our students with the opportunity to meet with success, but also a vision that is truly shared by all the stakeholders of our school. The No Child Left Behind Act's name in itself codifies the call to create schools to meet the ELCC and ISLLC's mantra of "promotes the success of all students."

The principle of benefit maximization also applies to the budgeting process. Our budgets must provide the greatest good for the most students. This means that tough decisions must be made. Tough decisions are not always popular decisions. But tough decisions made with integrity, fairness and in an ethical manner will propel our schools toward the fulfillment of our school vision. It is essential that the school budget be considered in tandem with the school vision.

The budget is an important tool in turning the vision into reality. When the budget process is divorced from the vision process, the likelihood of the vision being fulfilled dramatically decreases. Bracey (2002) provides a vivid illustration of what can happen when the budget process and the academic vision process are divorced. In his book, *The War Against America's Public Schools,* Bracey (2002) writes about a group of superintendents enthusiastically embracing a new efficiency model that changed them from scholars into managers. Bracey (2002) concludes his chiding of this particular efficiency model by writing, "Of course, one might wonder why, instead of studying ways to save money on toilet paper, superintendents didn't investigate why their charges dipped it in water and slung it at the walls" (p. 37).

When we consider this toilet paper problem from a purely accounting perspective we focus only on the financial cost associated with providing the toilet paper for student use and we neglect the possible academic issues at play in the misuse of the toilet paper. By only considering the financial issue associated with the use or misuse of the toilet paper, we wipe out the opportunity to get to the academic bottom of the toilet paper cost problem in terms of its cost to the school's vision to have all students meet with academic success. By including the academic perspective in conjunction with the budget perspective, hence the budget-vision connection, the toilet paper problem is then also considered as a potential indication of an academic failure to meet the needs of all students. Bottom line: budgeting and vision must be considered simultaneously if we are to reach our goal of 100% student success.

A second principle to consider in our examination of ethics is the Golden Rule. Many might mistakenly associate the Golden Rule with only the teachings of Jesus; however, there is some version of the Golden Rule in all of the major religions of the world. Table 2.3 provides a comparison of the Golden Rule in five of the world's major religions. The universal truth found in the Golden Rule is important to consider in our ethical treatment of others. It requires us to treat all people with equal value. People are entitled to equal opportunity. We must value all people and respect their educational goals. People must not be considered as merely assets to be used to achieve the school vision.

Finally, we must respect individual rights to make their own choices. When we include the Golden Rule as part of our code of ethics, we are more apt to integrate our budget process with our vision. We are less likely to see people as objects to be manipulated to achieve our own selfish purposes.

Table 2.3   Golden Rule in the World Religions

Religion	Golden Rule
Buddhism	Hurt not others in ways that you yourself would find hurtful. (Udana-Varga 5,1)
Christianity	All things whatsoever ye would that men should do to you, do ye so to them; for this is the law and the prophets. (Matthew 7:1)
Hinduism	This is the sum of duty; do naught unto others what you would not have them do unto you. (Mahabharata 5, 1517)
Islam	No one of you is a believer until he desires for his brother that which he desires for himself. (Sunah)
Judaism	What is hateful to you, do not do it to your fellowman. This is the entire Law; all the rest is commentary. (Talmud, Shabbat 3id)

SOURCE: University of the Golden Rule, http://teachingvalues.com/goldenrule. html

ELCC/ISLLC Standard 6

A school administrator is an educational leader who promotes the success of all students by understanding, responding to, and influencing the larger political, social, economic, legal, and cultural context.

We must approach our discussion of this standard from a global perspective. Intellectually we acknowledge that our schools do not operate in a vacuum. Yet we can get so caught up with the day-to-day demands of guiding our schools that we allow the big-picture to slip under the clutter on our desks. Standard 6 is a clarion call for us to understand our interconnectedness with each other and with the rest of the globe.

Our schools are interlaced in a myriad of political, social, economic, legal, and cultural ways at the local, state, national, and international levels in an increasingly complex and interconnected world. Accelerated technological developments have created dramatic social, political, and economic changes. The connectivity infrastructure with its DSL lines, cell phones, wireless technology, and high-speed modems are linking the planet together via the Internet. This explosion in the instantaneous sharing of information has had the effect of shrinking the globe and bringing the global village concept into a reality. Marshall

Figure 2.2   The Budgeting Food Chain

| World Economy | US Economy | State Economy | School Revenue |

Kathy Myrick, illustrator

McLuhan, who coined the term "global village," captured the impact of technology on our lives when he said, "Ours is a brand-new world of allatonceness [all-at-once-ness]. "Time' has ceased, 'space' has vanished. We now live in a global village . . . a simultaneous happening" (*Columbia*, 1996).

The American economy is part of a global economy as witnessed by the out-sourcing of American jobs overseas. Therefore, global events affect our economy; that, in turn, affects the amount of tax revenue that is available for public schools; that, in turn, impacts school budgets; and that, in turn, influences both the school planning and budgeting process. Wow! All of a sudden we feel like the end of a food chain (Figure 2.2)!

All said and done, Standard 6 reminds us that as we lead a school that promotes success for all students we are doing so within a global context, one in which both national and international events can impact the availability of funds for our school budget.

ELCC Standard 7

A school administrator is an educational leader who promotes the success of all students by substantial, sustained, standards-based experiences in real settings that are planned and guided cooperatively by university and school district personnel for graduate credit.

Your will recall that this ELCC standard is the only ELCC standard that does not have a corresponding ISLLC standard.

Standard 7 is the "odd duck" of the seven ELCC standards for school leaders. This observation is not meant to be negative nor derisive to this essential ELCC standard—just factual. This observation is meant to call attention to the fact that this standard is different in nature than the previous six ELCC/ISLLC standards. Maybe we can get out of trouble with the use of this odd duck descriptor by calling this standard the "ugly duckling" standard.

In the well-known children's story about the ugly duckling, the ugly duckling was different from all of his siblings and his adoptive parents. He did not quite fit in with the rest of his family. Initially, his differences from the rest of his family members made him a social outcast. Yet in the end the ugly duckling became a creature of beauty and was accepted by his whole family (Anderson, H.C., 1998). Like the ugly duckling, this standard is very different from its other six siblings, but we will argue the case for this standard and convince the reader that in reality, like the ugly duckling, it is really a creature of beauty.

Let's begin by examining this unique standard and how it ties into the budget-vision planning process. Face it, we cannot duck the issues embedded in this ELCC standard. Enough of this duck stuff!

Unlike the first six ELCC/ISLLC standards that draw upon the needs of all of the stakeholders in the educational process this ELCC standard focuses primarily on practicing and future school leaders. A casual glance at this standard returns a vision of self-indulgence on the part of present and future leaders. A long hard stare at this standard reveals not a self-serving image but an image of servant leader preparation. This internship-centered standard provides significant opportunities for the educator to synthesize and apply the knowledge and practice and develops the skills identified in ELCC/ISLLC Standards 1 through 6 (NPBEA, 2002).

ELCC Standard 7 poses a dilemma for the authors as we attempt to link it to the integrated school budget planning process premise of this book. This standard is related to the budget-vision relationship, but it will require that we go through a different door to confirm its connection. Each of the first six ELCC/ISLLC standards are directly associated to the budget-vision relationship. Standard 7, on the other hand, has the school leader as the primary participant with others in supportive roles. This reversal in role emphasis makes the budget-vision connection a step removed from the other six national standards. Although this ELCC standard is one step removed, it is still essential in the integrated budget planning process.

The structured, sustained, and standards based internship experience called for in this ELCC standard is essential for training school leaders to understand the budget-vision relationship. It is critical that educational leaders be provided with the opportunity to apply the knowledge and skills described in the previous standards in a workplace setting. The resources required to accomplish this standard, although budgeted initially to a narrowly defined audience and subject to criticism as self-serving, will in the future provide a return on the investment manyfold greater. School leaders who understand the national standards support of integrating budget and vision in the planning process are much more likely to lead their schools to achieve the "academic success for all students" call imbedded in the national standards.

Final Thoughts

School budgeting and vision must be considered simultaneously in the planning process in order for schools to increase their likelihood of achieving the Utopian goal of "all students meeting with success." The ELCC/ISLLC standards provide the guideposts that are necessary for school leaders to facilitate academic success for all.

The trick is for school leaders to incorporate the generalities of the national standards into practical steps to achieve the ideal of academic success for all students. This chapter at times might appear to be "Pollyannaish." Some of the examples and metaphors could illicit a "pie in the sky" reaction from the reader. However, it is important for us to begin the integrated budget planning process with a "pie in the sky" perspective. To do otherwise would immediately lower our expectation to less than 100% of the students obtaining academic success. 99.9% is not good enough. If 99.9% was good enough, then 12 babies would be given to the wrong parents each day, two planes landing daily at O'Hare International Airport would be unsafe, and 291 pacemaker operations would be performed incorrectly this year (Godwords, n.d.).

Covey (1990) encourages school leaders to begin with the end in mind. Our end in mind is 100% of our students meeting with the academic success called for in each of the national standards using an integrated approach to budgeting process. There are many forces working against school leaders in achieving this goal. In the remaining chapters greater specificity will be provided to help us obtain the 100% expectation.

Discussion Questions

1. Which one of the national standards do you think influences the budget-vision relationship the most in your situation? Why?

2. Do you agree or disagree with the authors' contention that we "must visit Utopia" in creating a vision for our schools or is this just "fluff"? Support your response.

3. How have you witnessed the shift from technical skills to interpersonal skills? Support your answer.

4. How have you witnessed the shift from director to consensus builder and motivator?

5. How have you witnessed the shift from resource allocation to accountability?

6. What are your initial thoughts on the author's contention that budgeting and vision must be integrated in the planning process in order to promote the success of all students?

7. Have you been a part of or witnessed a situation similar to the budget-vision disconnect toilet paper problem? If so, relate your experience.

Case Study Application: Belle Plain Middle School

Belle Plain Middle School (BPMS) is comprised of approximately 1,000 students in grades 6 through 8. The school is 40% Anglo, 25% Hispanic, 25% African American, 5% Asian American, and 5% other. Of these students, 60% qualify for free or reduced lunch; 12% of the students are identified as limited English proficient; the campus mobility rate is 30%.

The facility is 25 years old and is in an average state of repair. The neighborhood around the school is comprised of modest homes of a similar age to the school. Many homes are in good repair and evidence pride in ownership. Most of the nearby businesses are independently owned small businesses. There is the typical scattering of franchised fast-food restaurants.

The majority of parents of the students at BPMS are employed in blue-collar jobs. A recently constructed subdivision of upper-middle-class homes in the attendance zone has created the potential of changing the campus demographics. The super majority of students who reside in the new subdivision are either being home-schooled or are enrolled in a private school 20 minutes away because of parent concerns about the academic integrity of Belle Plain Middle School. The parents from this subdivision who have enrolled their children in the school want to meet with the principal about becoming more involved in the school and in their children's education.

The BPMS faculty is divided into two groups. The Old Pros are those teachers who have an average experience of more than 15 years at the school. The Green Horns are comprised of faculty and staff who have less than five years experience at the school. The latter group has a high turnover rate. There is tension between the two faculty groups as well as a certain amount of distrust. The Old Pros perceive the Green Horns as short on experience and long on idealism. The Green Horns perceive the Old Pros as jaded and insensitive to the needs of the students. They also accuse the Old Pros of being unwilling to attempt innovative strategies to meet the student needs because of professional bias.

A total of 65% of all students passed the state reading test. The passing rate for Hispanics and African Americans was 52%; Limited English Proficient students had a 47% passing rate on the state reading test. Percentages who passed the state mathematics test were: 71% of all students; 59% of the Hispanics passed the mathematics test; 61percent of the African American students; and 53% of the Limited English Proficient students passed the mathematics test.

The percent of students identified as needing special education services is 17% above the state average. The percentage of Hispanic students in special education is 53% higher than the Anglo rate.

You are the new principal on the campus. You are the third principal in five years. The selection process for hiring you was substantially different from that used with previous principals. The superintendent secured a search committee comprised of parents, teachers, staff, and community members. A successful effort was made to involve individuals of all ethnic and socio-economic groups. The superintendent screened the initial applicant list and submitted the names of five individuals for the committee to interview and make a recommendation to him. The two male and three female finalists were ethnically diverse. Like you, all of the finalists were from outside the school district.

The superintendent and board have set a priority of turning Belle Plain Middle School around. You have been promised a 12% increase in your campus budget for the next three years. The campus has also been allotted two additional faculty positions to be determined by you in a collaborative effort with the faculty and staff.

The previous two principals gave lip service to involving teachers and staff in making academic plans for the students. A campus academic improvement plan was developed each year but was never referred to during the school year. The previous principals usually made some modifications to the previous year's plan and ran it by the faculty for a quick vote before sending it to the superintendent.

Teachers have little or no knowledge about the campus budget. They are not aware of what financial resources are available to the campus. Currently, the primary way of securing financial resources is to ask the principal and wait until a response is received.

Three years ago the parent-teacher organization was abandoned for lack of attendance. The superintendent has informed you that the two Hispanic board members receive frequent complaints that Hispanic parents do not feel welcome or valued on the campus. A recent parent survey compiled by the central administration indicates, among other things, that many of the Old Pros believe their students are not performing well because the children do not try hard enough and the parents do not care.

Application Questions

1. How can you as the principal promote the success of all students at Belle Plain Middle School by facilitating the development, articulation, implementation, and stewardship of a school vision of learning that will be shared and supported by the school community?

2. How can you as the principal promote the success of all students at Belle Plain Middle School by advocating, nurturing, and sustaining a school culture and instructional program conducive to student learning and staff professional growth?

3. How can you as principal of Belle Plain Middle School promote the success of all students by ensuring management of the schools operations and budget for a safe, efficient, and effective learning environment?

4. How can you promote success of all students by collaborating with families and community members, responding to the diverse community interests and needs of Belle Plain Middle School, and mobilize the community resources?

5. How can you as the principal promote success of all the students at Belle Plain Middle School by acting with integrity, fairness, and in an ethical manner?

6. How can you as principal promote the success of all students by understanding, responding to, and influencing the larger political, economic, legal, and cultural context of Belle Plain Middle School?

7. Is there additional information that is not provided that you think would be beneficial in addressing the issues raised in the first six questions? If so what information is needed and why?

---

1. These standards are reprinted with permission from *Interstate School Leaders Licensure Consortium (ISLLC) standards for school leaders*, (1996). Washington, DC: Council of Chief State School Officers. The Interstate School Leaders Licensure Consortium (ISLLC) Standards were developed by the Council of Chief School Officers (CCSSO) and member states. Copies may be downloaded from the Council's Web site at www.ccsso.org.

3

School Culture & Using Data Effectively

We live in a culture that has come to value and depend on statistical information to inform our decisions. At the same time we are likely to misunderstand and misuse those statistics because we are "statistically illiterate" and consequently have no idea what the numbers mean.

—Lorna Earl

The trip to Utopia provided us with a clear view of the ideal world we are seeking for our schools. Unfortunately, we do not live in an ideal world. Rather, we live in a world filled with many challenges such as shortages of financial and physical resources; and we serve an ever-growing and increasingly diverse student population. In an opinion column, George Will commented on the challenges of constructing the federal government budget when he penned, "'Anyone,' said T.S. Eliot, 'could carve a goose were it not for the bones.' Anyone could write a sensible federal budget, were it not for the bones—the sturdy skeleton of existing programs defended by muscular interests" (Will, 2005). The same can be said about the integrated school budget process. When school leaders become serious about aligning the school budget with the school vision, they can expect to encounter the sturdy skeleton of existing programs as they attempt to carve a budget aligned with the school's vision. The bones of programs near and dear to some stakeholders will not necessarily be germane to attaining the school's vision. Besides the bones of existing programs, school leaders can also expect bones of impaired vision from stockholders who either do not understand or choose not to accept the academic success for all as exemplified in Ron Edmonds remark, "We can, whenever we want, successfully teach all children whose schooling is of interest to us. We already know more than we need to do that. Whether or not we do it must depend on how we feel about the fact that we haven't so far" (Edmonds, 1979, p. 56). Let us examine the importance of the role of school culture, data, and assessment on the development of an integrated budget.

School Culture

The importance of a school culture receptive to the integrated budget model purported in this book cannot be overemphasized. Wilkins and Paterson (1985) remind us: "Culture consists of the conclusions a group of people draws from its experience. An organization's [school's] culture consists largely of what people believe about what works and what does not" (p. 5). Integrating the budget and vision into a single process cannot flourish unless it is woven into the fabric of the school's culture. The integrated budget model requires a school culture receptive to collaboration. Schools, which possess a collegial spirit, create the required collaborative environment that in turn increases enthusiasm, energy, and motivation (Dorsch, 1998). This integration must be valued by the school's culture and at the same time serve as a vehicle to turn dreams into reality.

We touched upon school culture in our examination of ELCC/ISLLC Standard 2 in chapter two. Standard 2 calls on school leaders to "promote success of all students by advocating, nurturing, and sustaining a school culture and instructional program conducive to student learning and staff professional growth." This national standard warrants closer examination because the integrated budget process cannot exist with any degree of usefulness unless it is inculcated into the school's culture.

Kilmann, Saxton, and Serpa (1985) defined culture as "the shared philosophies, ideologies, values, assumptions, beliefs, expectations, attitudes, and norms that knit a community together" (p. 5). The community is our school. Kilmann et al.'s use of the adjective *shared* in defining culture is of importance when considering it with the ELCC/ISLLC Standard 2 edict that educational leaders *promote* a school culture. *Shared* is a WE thing. Shared implies that all of the stakeholders in the school hold core values in common. *Promote* requires us as school leaders to take the initiative to advocate, nourish, and sustain the school culture in such a manner that we meet the edict of Standard 2.

We will briefly examine three elements of school culture—values, beliefs, and attitudes—as we state our case for making the integration of budget and vision a part of every school's culture. We will conduct this examination within our ELCC/ISLLC obligation to advocate, nourish, and sustain the school culture.

Values

Values are those things we hold near and dear. They are the things that we deem important. Values shape the practice of teachers and staff (Nash, 1996). For the integrated approach to budgeting to become a part of a school's culture, stakeholders must understand how this approach can help them reach their personal mission as well as the school's vision. As leaders we must advocate the integrated approach to budgeting when we support it, plead its case, and assist the stakeholders in understanding it. We nurture it by discussing it in formal and informal team meetings and by sharing it with parents and community members. We sustain it by never letting it be removed from the conscious of our stakeholders.

Beliefs

Beliefs are what we hold to be true. The integrated relationship between budget, vision, and planning must become something that the stakeholders hold to be true. Gradually, through time and effort and by constantly keeping the integrated budget process at the core of school planning, events will unfold and stories will develop that will become a part of the school's heritage. Some stories will be rooted in embellished accomplishments that occurred through the integrated budgetary process. Rituals will manifest themselves as ceremonies. Deal and Kennedy (1982) say that ceremonies are to culture what movies are to scripts. They afford the players an opportunity to act out their beliefs. Ceremonies can become ongoing events that sustain the integrated budget approach in the school culture.

Attitudes

Attitudes are how we feel about things. Over time, the school's stakeholders must feel that the school cannot function at its best unless the integrated budget approach is at the core of the school's planning process. The more the integrated process is used in planning, the more deep-seated it becomes as part of the school's culture. Kilmann et al. (1985) aptly phrased an attitude that develops: "[That's] the way things are done around here" (p. 5). It takes time for ideas to become part of the school's culture. Ebullient leaders never tire in their effort to advocate and nurture the budget-vision-planning relationship for it to be incorporated as a part of the culture. We must never cease in our effort; we must constantly strive to sustain it as part of who we are.

Data-Driven Decision Making

The Sorenson-Goldsmith Integrated Budget Model (Figure 4.1, p. 65) is introduced in the next chapter. The third and fourth components of this model involve data gathering and data analysis. We might be getting the proverbial cart before the horse, but we are compelled to call special attention to data gathering and analysis before we introduce the model. It's okay to look ahead and take a peek at the model.

Effective use of data will change a school's culture. Data can be used to expose our bias and ignorance, it can provide us with "Aha!" moments, as well as debunk ineffective practices. In short, data gathering and analysis can be the catalyst for changing the school's culture for the good.

The authors have personal experience in using data to expose ineffective teaching practices. Ineffective practices left alone and unchallenged become encoded within the school's culture. To be fair, we must not think that ineffective practices are deliberately adopted with the intent to harm or limit student achievement or potential. This said, whether ineffective instructional practices are unintentional or intentional, the results are the same—low performance for students AND teachers, low expectations, and a drag on the school's culture.

Both authors had the opportunity to affect school culture by using data to end the practice of ability grouping. Providing our faculties with longitudinal as well as disaggregated data on student achievement made it apparent to the stakeholders that this system of teaching was only widening the gap between the various subpopulations on our campuses. This data "Aha!" could not be refuted by anecdotal arguments by those attempting to cling to this failed instructional strategy. The dismantling of ability groups began. A culture of data decision making also planted a foothold in the school's culture.

As time passed, both campuses matured in incorporating data within the decision-making process. This was evidenced by stakeholders seeking additional sources of data. As the use of data-driven decisions increased on the campus, so did the level of teacher expectations for all students. No longer were faculty and staff content with whole school academic performance data. There was an expectation for achievement data to be disaggregated into the appropriate subpopulations. This analysis of data sparked imaginations as interventions were being formulated to improve the performance of any subpopulation that did not achieve to the campus expectations.

As data gathering and analysis continued their mercurial rise in value by the school's culture so did the concept of continuous incremental improvement. This was a good thing. No longer would the school be satisfied with maintaining the status quo. The school was now committed to continuous improvement.

One example of this commitment was in the area of student achievement. One group of teachers who had been using data-driven decision making for several years were consistently witnessing their student mastery on the state reading examination fall between the 90% to even the 100% passing rate. This group of teachers took their data analysis to the next level. They began examining not only *if* their students passed the reading exam, but *how well* they passed the exam. This led to a higher self-imposed level of expectation for student achievement. The academic goal would no longer be limited to the passing rate of the exam but also to how well the students passed the state's reading exam.

This story is not over. These teachers did not stop at this level of data analysis. They continued their analysis of student subpopulation performance by reading objective. However, they added an analysis of the student wrong answers to questions. They used this analysis to determine where they needed to refine the delivery of instruction to help the students master the reading curriculum. When data-driven decision making is valued, watch out! The sky's the limit with regard to where a school can go.

Barriers to the Use of Data

Edie L. Holcomb (2004) identifies six reasons why data are little used and why it is a challenge to motivate people to be data driven. Holcomb's barriers in the use of data are:

- Lack of proper training in involving others in decision making and in the appropriate use of decision making.
- Lack of time.
- Feast or famine—fearing that there is no data or panicking over too much: what are we going to do with all these data?
- Fear of evaluation—that the data is going to be used against individuals or schools.
- Fear of exposure—the fear that even though your colleagues believe you are a good teacher, the data might expose you as a fraud.
- Confusing a technical problem with a cultural problem.

Holcomb (2004) reminds us that collecting data for the sake of collecting data is an exercise in futility "unless it engages people by connecting to the deep and authentic passion for teaching and learning" (p. xxi).

Ruth Johnson (2002) effectively describes five stages in the change process for creating stakeholders valuing the incorporation of data gathering and analysis into the decision-making process. Briefly those steps are:

1. *Building the Leadership and Data Teams.* A recognition develops that data must be used in the reform process. Training is provided on the skills needed to collect and analyze data.

2. *Killing the Myth/Building Dissatisfaction.* Data are used to reveal false beliefs about educational practices such as having low expectations for certain groups of students.

3. *Creating a Culture of Inquiry.* School values provocative questioning and responses that use data to inspire the school change process.

4. *Creating a Vision and Plan for Your School.* This stage requires a long-term collaborative planning process that will result in positive change. It involves establishing priorities, allocating resources, and assigning responsibilities.

5. *Monitoring Progress.* Monitoring becomes a part of the school culture.

Both Holcomb's and Johnson's books are superior resources in providing the technical expertise in implementing the third and fourth components of the Sorenson-Goldsmith Integrated Budget Model discussed in Chapter 4.

Dimensions of Data

This section calls attention to the nature and necessity of data-driven decisions in the integrated budget process. However, we cannot do justice to this important concept within the confines of this book. Data-driven decision-making skills must be acquired in order to effectively use the integrated budget model. Two premier sources on data gathering and analysis have already been identified. An additional list of excellent resources is located at the end of this chapter to assist in the mastery of data-associated skills.

W. Edwards Deming believes that "Quality comes not from inspection but from improvement of the process" (Walton, 1986, p. 60). We improve the process when we improve the quality of the data used in our decision making. Good decision making is only as good as the data used in formulating the decisions. The challenge for school leaders today is to sift through mountains of information to construct informed decisions. The dilemma we face in this process is that schools are about the business of students, and students' needs cannot always be easily described, plotted, and analyzed on spreadsheets.

Federal legislation such as the No Child Left Behind Act of 2001 as well as state legislation aimed at increasing education accountability requires us to use new data sources. Laffee (2002) writes, "The tools of education—intuition, teaching philosophy, personal experience—do not seem to be enough anymore. Virtually every state has put into place an assessment system intended to measure and validate student achievement and school performance" (p. 6). School leaders need to not only possess the three skills that Laffee references, they must go beyond them.

Types of Data

Today's school leader must employ a variety of data sources. These data come in five basic types: disaggregated data, longitudinal data, perception data, qualitative data, and quantitative data (see Table 3.1). Each of these data types provides its own unique assistance in developing an integrated budget.

Disaggregated Data

Disaggregated data are data broken down by specific student subgroups such as current grade, race, previous achievements, gender, and socioeconomic status. Disaggregated data provide leaders with an additional level of specificity needed to identify the academic

Table 3.1 Types of Data

Data Type	Definition
Disaggregated	Data broken down by specific student subgroups such as current grade, race, previous achievements, gender, and socioeconomic status.
Longitudinal	Data measured consistently from year to year to track progress, growth, and change over time. True longitudinal studies eliminate any students who were not present and were not tested in each of the years of the study.
Perception	Data that inform educators about parent, student, and staff perceptions about the learning environment, which could also reveal areas in need of improvement.
Qualitative	Data based on information gathered from one-on-one interviews, focus groups, or general observations over time (as opposed to quantitative data).
Quantitative	Data based on "hard numbers" such as enrollment figures, dropout rates, and test scores (as opposed to qualitative data).

SOURCE: From *Using Data to Improve Schools: What's Working* by AASA, 2002.

needs of schools. A fictitious academic example of the Langtry B. Jensen Middle School is provided to illustrate the importance of disaggregated data. Table 3.2 displays student achievement disaggregated by grade, race, and economic status. For the sake of brevity, we truncated the display to only two years of data and limited it to two areas of the curriculum.

Instead of examining student achievement data from a whole school population perspective, we now have the opportunity to examine the student academic performance by ethnicity as well as socioeconomic status. For example, if we examine the 2005 seventh-grade reading scores we see that the campus had a passing rate of 83% which was 1% higher than the state passing rate of 82%. Our initial reaction might be one of academic smugness, believing that we were performing above the state average in seventh-grade reading. But by employing disaggregated data we can recognize that there are some problems in the reading program. Whites passed at the rate of 93%, Hispanics at 77%, and the low socioeconomic status group at 72%. The 16 to 21 percentage points lower performance of the latter two subpopulations provide us with priority and academic direction

Table 3.2   Langtry B. Jensen Middle School State Academic Performance

	State	District	Campus	African American	Hispanic	White	Low SES
				All numbers are in percent			
Met State Standard: Grade 6							
Reading							
2006	87	83	86	*	84	89	82
2005	80	76	83		80	88	74
Mathematics							
2006	78	65	80	*	77	84	73
2005	71	61	65		64	68	53
Met State Standard: Grade 7							
Reading							
2006	83	79	94	*	92	98	94
2005	82	78	83		77	93	72
Mathematics							
2006	71	60	71	*	69	76	69
2005	63	52	57		52	69	43
Met State Standard: Grade 8							
Reading							
2006	90	88	94	*	89	99	84
2005	84	79	86		83	93	75
Mathematics							
2006	67	57	83	*	76	92	72
2005	62	50	48		44	55	38

* Less than 10 students.

as to where we need to intervene. The use of disaggregated data assisted us in identifying an instructional delivery problem that we would not have seen had we not used disaggregated data.

Longitudinal Data

Longitudinal data are data measured consistently from year to year to track progress, growth, and change over time. True longitudinal studies eliminate any students who were not present and tested in each of the years of the study. When we return to Table 3.2 we realize that not only does it contain disaggregated data, it also contains longitudinal data. Once again for the sake of brevity, our example contains only two years of data. In an actual school situation we would want to have five or so years of data if at all possible. As we examine these data for 2005 and 2006 we can see significant improvement in several areas. One example is the sixth-grade mathematics scores for low socioeconomic students. In 2005, 53% of the students passed the mathematics test compared to 73% in 2006. This was an increase of 20 percentage points. Another way to examine these data is to return to the low socioeconomic sixth-grade students' mathematics score in 2005 of 53% and compare it to the low socioeconomic seventh-grade student mathematics scores of 2006 which were 69%. By comparing the scores in this manner we are following relatively the same group of students over a two-year period. This analysis reveals a growth of 16 percentage points between 2005 and 2006 in this same group comparison. By using sophisticated software, school leaders can more readily construct longitudinal comparisons of same groups from year to year, which, in turn, provides guidance to areas of curriculum and instruction that need to be adjusted.

Perception Data

Perception data are data that inform educators about parent, student, and staff perceptions regarding the learning environment, which could also reveal areas in need of improvement. An example of perception data collection is a parent survey conducted by the school planning committee at L. B. Jensen Middle School. Table 3.3 contains a summary of the responses to 3 of 35 questions in the L. B. Jensen Middle School Parent Survey. Parents were asked to respond to the questions by circling a number on a scale of 1 to 4 (1 strongly agree, 2 agree, 3 disagree, 4 strongly disagree). The results for 2005 and 2006 are included in Table 3.3. It should be noted that 61% of the parents responded to the survey in 2005 and 62% responded in 2006.

Table 3.3   L. B. Jensen Middle School Parent Survey Results (Abridged)

Question	Response	2005, %	2006, %
If I were given a voucher and could enroll	1	82	92
my child at any other middle school	2	2	2
I would still enroll my child at	3	3	4
L.B. Jensen MS.	4	11	2
The reading program at L.B. Jensen MS	1	77	89
is a good program for my child.	2	4	8
	3	7	3
	4	12	0
The mathematics program at L.B. Jensen	1	66	82
MS is a good program for my child.	2	4	3
	3	10	8
	4	20	7

Since Table 3.3 contains more than one year of survey results, not only are the data perceptive data, but are also longitudinal and quantitative data. One observation that can be drawn from these data is that the parents have a more positive perception of the mathematics program in 2006 than they did in 2005. We could go another step further and return to Table 3.2 and note that during this same time period there was also a corresponding significant improvement in student performance in mathematics.

Qualitative Data

Qualitative data are data based on information gathered from one-on-one interviews, focus groups or general observations over time (as opposed to quantitative data). One example of qualitative data is when a school district brings in focus groups to discuss a controversial topic such as sex education. The district compiles the comments from the sessions and uses it in conjunction with information from other sources to revise its sex education program.

Quantitative Data

Quantitative data are data based on "hard numbers" such as enrollment figures, dropout rates, and test scores (as opposed to qualitative data). If we reference back once again to Table 3.2 we realize it contains the reporting of test scores. This means that the data are quantitative data. Two earlier examinations revealed that the data in Table 3.2 were also disaggregated data as well as longitudinal data. Data can meet the definition of more than one category of data.

Assessment

There are two basic types of assessment: formative and summative. Formative assessment is "assessment in which learning is measured at several points during a teaching/learning phase, with the primary intention of obtaining information to guide the further teaching or learning steps. Formative assessments include questioning, comments on a presentation or interviewing" (AASA, 2002, p. 68). An example of formative assessment is a pretest given in an academic area such as algebra, reading comprehension, or keyboarding skills. This information would then be used to drive the instructional strategy and the development of lesson plans.

The second type of assessment is summative. Summative assessment is "an assessment at the end of a period of education or training that sums up how a student has performed" (AASA, 2002, p. 70). An example of summative assessment is a post-test given in algebra, reading comprehension, or keyboarding to determine mastery of objectives. Formative and summative assessment when planned properly can yield all five types of data discussed earlier. Formative and summative data used in conjunction with each other is invaluable in making program adjustments.

Final Thoughts

School cultures can change. We must: (1) involve all the stakeholders treating them with dignity and respect; (2) be results oriented while being data driven; (3) constantly monitor our school culture; (4) see possibilities and not problems; (5) assure that our efforts are ongoing; and (6) see the value of everyone in our school. We are more likely to achieve these and other goals when we put our money where our mouth is and align our budget and commit our resources to the vision of our school. The best way we can make our school successful is to create a culture that influences all our stakeholders to adopt, by tacit agreement, the most effective approach, attitude, and behavior while at the school (Kilmann, et al., 1985).

Discussion Questions

1. What are some good data sources for schools to use in decision making?

2. What data sources have you utilized in decision making?

3. How have you witnessed the use of technology in providing and analyzing data?

4. What is the connection between the chapter and the quote from Lorna Earl at the beginning of the chapter?

5. What are ways that school leaders can advocate, nurture, and sustain the school's culture?

6. How would you describe the culture of your current school?

7. Has there been a school you particularly enjoyed or disliked? If so how would you describe its culture?

8. Describe ways you have used formative and summative data?

Case Study Application: L. B. Jensen Middle School

L. B. Jensen Middle School, a school of 540 students in grades six through eight is located in a southern border state less than 200 miles from the U.S.–Mexico border. It is 62% Hispanic and 38% Anglo. It is one of six middle schools in Kilnwood City. Juan Quervo is the principal of L. B. Jensen MS. Although L. B. Jensen MS has always been predominantly Hispanic, Dr. Quervo is the first Hispanic to be named as the principal of L. B. Jensen MS in its 42 years of existence. Dr. Quervo has been enthusiastically accepted by all of the school's stakeholders. He is using this acceptance capital to make needed instructional changes to insure that all children meet with academic success.

Table 3.2 contains two years accumulation of achievement data for L. B. Jensen Middle School. Table 3.3 contains a partial report on the responses to the parent survey for the last two school years. Use these data to respond to the following questions.

Application Questions

1. Using the data provided, identify at least two instructional concerns at L. B. Jensen Middle School. What types of data did you use to identify the concerns?

2. Using the data provided, what would you recommend to Dr. Quervo as the top instructional priority? Support your recommendation with data.

3. There was a noted increase in the positive perception of L. B. Jensen MS by the parents between 2005 and 2006. Is there anything in the given data that might explain the recent upward swing in the campus's public perception? Support your response

4. What data are not provided that you would like to have to be better informed about the needs and strengths of understanding L. B. Jensen MS?

5. What other data would be useful in determining the reason(s) for the improvement of the mathematics and reading scores?

Other Resources

American Association of School Administrators (2002). *Using data to improve schools: What's working.* Alexandria, VA: AASA.

Bernhardt, V. L. (2003). *Using data to improve student learning in elementary schools.* Larchmont, NY: Eye on Education.

Bernhardt, V. L. (2004). *Using data to improve student learning in middle schools.* Larchmont, NY: Eye on Education.

Bernhardt, V. L. (2005). *Using data to improve student learning in high schools.* Larchmont, NY: Eye on Education.

Bracey, G. W. (2000). *Bail me out!: Handling difficult data and tough questions about public schools.* Thousand Oaks, CA: Corwin.

Creighton, T. B. (2001). *Schools and data: The educator's guide for using data to improve decision making.* Thousand Oaks, CA: Corwin.

Holcomb, E. L. (2004). *Getting excited about data* (2nd ed.). Thousand Oaks, CA: Corwin.

Johnson, R. S. (2002). *Using data to close the achievement gap: How to measure equity in our schools* (2nd ed.). Thousand Oaks, CA: Corwin.

Odden, A. & Archibald, S. (2001). *Reallocating resources: How to boost student achievement without asking for more.* Thousand Oaks, CA: Corwin.

4

A Model for Integrating Vision, Planning, and Budgeting

I learned over and over again that the relationship among the adults in the schoolhouse has more impact on the quality and the character of the school—and on the accomplishments of youngsters—than any other factor.

—Roland Barth

We began our examination of the integration of the vision, budgeting, and planning processes by delineating between school finance and school budgeting. From that point, we examined the relationship that budgeting has with each of the ELCC/ISLLC standards. We then completed a closer examination of the budgeting and vision relationship with an emphasis on culture, climate, and data-driven decision making. It is now time to allow these underlying principles to manifest themselves into a practical and workable model of operation.

Figure 4.1   Sorenson-Goldsmith Integrated Budget Model

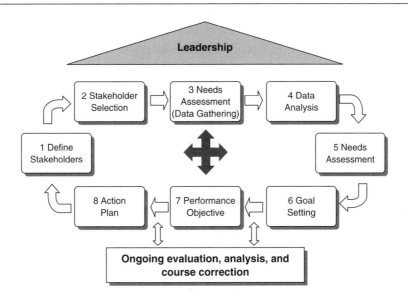

Figure 4.1 provides us with an illustration of such a model. It will be necessary to consider each component of the Sorenson-Goldsmith Integrated Budget Model individually to ensure a thorough understanding of the integrative nature of this model. This model is based on many of the principles associated with the site-based decision-making (SBDM) process. The SBDM process, a collaborative process using stakeholders within the organization, is required in Colorado, Florida, Kentucky, North Carolina, and Texas in some form. It is also used in districts throughout the United States (Clover, Jones, Bailey, and Griffin, 2004). This process can function at either the campus or district level. The term *school* in the remainder of this chapter refers to either a campus or a district. The level of planning in which the Sorenson-Goldsmith model is being utilized determines which definition of school is employed.

Sorenson-Goldsmith Integrated Budget Model

Leadership

Leadership is located at the top of the model, not to symbolize top-down leadership, but rather to represent the relational leadership exhibited between a shepherd and the sheep. For centuries shepherds have tended flocks in isolated areas. The shepherd assisted in meeting a host of needs of the sheep through service and openness that produced trusting relationships. Shepherds fed their sheep, found water for them and protected them from wild animals. If a sheep got lost, a shepherd looked for it. The shepherd knew each lamb in his flock by name. Shepherds did not walk behind the sheep, they led them. Likewise, the sheep recognized the shepherd's voice and touch (Anderson, L., 1997). School leaders must provide this same type of relationship and communication as we assist and nurture the collaborative planning process.

Traditional leadership might produce positive results—but at a cost to the collaborative planning process. Decisions may be made in an orderly meeting run with firm control, but apathy and resentment may be the price to be paid (Yukl, 2001).

Communication is a necessary leadership skill in working with the school planning committee. The school leader must communicate passion for the mission of the school. The leader must kindle the imagination of all the stakeholders about what can be done to help the school achieve its vision and mission. A leader cannot be a visionary without being persuasive. The school planning committee must witness the leader's passion for the school.

Leaders must foster the crafting of a clear vision for the school, one that resonates with all of its stakeholders. Leaders must believe that the committee members want to be inspired to help fulfill the school's vision. It is incumbent on leaders to provide stakeholders with opportunities to envision, understand, and experience the school's vision as they develop a school action plan using this model. Vision is not free. It costs time, money, and energy. Each of the components of this model will be individually examined in an effort to help bring our visions into realities.

Component 1: Defining Stakeholders

If the entire learning community is to have ownership in the school site-based decision-making process, then it must commence by giving consideration to all of the various stakeholders of the community. Some expected stakeholders include:

- Teachers
- Staff members
- Business
- Other professionals

- Administration
- Parents
- Community members
- Students

Each of these stakeholders is valuable to the planning process for each brings a unique perspective.

Teachers are the classroom teachers who are in daily contact with students. Staff members refer to those who are noncertified employees. They include but are not limited to paraprofessionals and custodians. Other professionals are degreed individuals such as counselors, nurses, and educational diagnosticians. Administration refers to the campus and central office administrators. Parents are those who have guardianship over the children who attend the public schools. Finally, community members are people who live in the community but who have no child in the public school system.

It is important to note that the majority of households in this country do not have children in the public schools, yet the schools must seek and gain their support if school funding and bonds are to be enacted into law. It is imperative that this group of stakeholders be represented in the planning process.

Component 2: Selection of Stakeholders

An examination of state and local policies is appropriate to ensure compliance with any state laws or regulations in selecting stakeholders. Local policies and administrative procedures must be put into place to determine the structure and authority of the school collaborative planning committee. Procedures should also be established that define the roles and responsibilities of the committee.

Committee Size and Structure

The size and structure of the collaborative planning committee must be considered. The authors believe that teachers should comprise somewhere between a majority to super-majority of the committee positions. The election and selection of committee members should be as simple as possible. While it might serve well to elect faculty and staff committee positions, it would be more efficient if other positions, such as parents and community members, were appointed. Once again, clear procedures must be in place.

Diversity

Careful consideration should be given to creating diversity on the committee in the selection of appointed committee members. Appointments should represent the community's diversity. Besides ethnic diversity, other populations should be represented. Parent representatives should also reflect the diverse needs of the school's students. Among those populations to be considered are parents of children who:

- Speak English as a second language
- Have special needs
- Have special gifts and talents
- Come from a variety of socioeconomic situations

There are several actions administrators can take to increase the diversity of the SBDM committee. Chief among those actions are:

- Advertising in the local newspaper
- Securing public service announcements on local television and radio stations
- Seeking nominations from the PTAs or PTOs
- Seeking nominations from local businesses
- Seeking nominations from community organizations such at the Chamber of Commerce or Kiwanis Club

Members who are nominated should be willing to serve and be willing to invest the time in the school's planning process. This is not the time for arms to be twisted.

The administrator or selection committee who finalizes the selection of these school planning committee members needs to deliberate conscientiously over the nominations. It is paramount that the intent of ELCC/ISLLC Standard 5, the ethics standard, bathe this process. Some questions to be considered are:

- Does this individual have the time to attend committee meetings?
- Will this individual be willing to attend training on the committee?
- Does this person demonstrate a willingness to listen to all sides of an issue?

Committee Member Training

Committee members need to be trained to understand their role in the collaborative decision-making process. McCloskey, Mikow-Porto, and Bingham (1998) reveal that frequently principals and faculty members have not been trained adequately to meet with success in the collaborative planning process. The committee needs designated areas to examine budgeting, curriculum, staffing patterns, staff development, and school organization if it is to improve school performance (Odden & Wohlsletter, 1995). These areas need to be clearly defined in the training process. This will prevent misunderstandings about the committee's function and authority.

Committee members should also receive training in team building skills. Committee members should develop their listening skills, understand other cultures, and know how to use conflict resolution skills. Finally, training must be provided in the collection and interpretation of data. The committee must be convinced of the merits of using data as the basis for creating change in the school (Earl & Katz, 2005).

Staggering the Terms

Consideration should be given to staggering the terms for committee members. This technique will ensure stability and experience over time. If members serve two-year terms then at least 50% of the school planning committee would be experienced members at any given time.

Component 3: Needs Assessment (Data Gathering)

We got a head start on discussing data gathering in Chapter 3. Like businesses, schools are now expected to verify their performance with solid data. The No Child Left Behind Act has only added new responsibilities for schools to gather, collect, and analyze data from a wide range of sources. Federal law now requires state education agencies to report student performance by income, English fluency, migrant status, race, gender, and disability. The increased pressure for external accountability has heightened the need for schools to be data-driven (Harris, 2004; Laffee, 2002). Gathering data is essential for developing goals. Fullan (1991) emphasized that the success of the school's program is dependent on how efficiently data is collected on measuring the change being implemented in the school.

Needs assessment requires the school planning committee to ponder, "How well is our school doing in meeting the goals of our school improvement plan?" The answer to this question must go beyond the hunches and feelings of the committee members. No longer can schools simply proclaim, "We had a great year. Our students made tremendous progress." The answer to this question requires the committee to gather data from an array of sources in order to complete a comprehensive assessment. The more data collected from a broad range of sources, the greater the likelihood that the committee will accurately respond to the posed question.

Philip Streifer, a superintendent, accurately described data collection when he said, "Data collection is a messy, messy business. It is done in different formats, sometimes electronically, sometimes on cards or paper, often it's incomplete. Teachers collect it differently and not everybody has the same access to it, which means not everybody is going to be on the same page" (Laffee, 2002, p. 7). Data can originate from a variety of sources. The following list provides some great sources for collecting data on a school.

- Student achievement test results
- Attendance data (student and faculty)
- Dropout data
- School budget reports
- Parent surveys
- Student surveys
- Faculty surveys
- Focus groups
- Volunteer logs
- Transfer requests (student and faculty)
- Retention data
- Failure reports
- Discipline data
- Facilities report
- Organizational description (mission, vision, values)
- Staff development needs
- Staffing patterns
- Accident reports
- Extracurricular data
- Special populations data
- Mobility rate
- Unusual events on the campus (i.e., death of a student, fire, shooting, etc.)
- Any other information useful in measuring the school's performance

As data is gathered, a school profile begins to emerge. This profile reflects the school's operating environment, key educational programs, resource allocation, and other facets of the school. Once the data is gathered, the committee is then ready to sift through the information to derive meaning out of the sea of numbers and reports.

Needs assessment does not cease with the gathering of information. It must go to the next step—data analysis.

Component 4: Data Analysis

We began our discussion of measurement, analysis, and management of data as keys to improving student performance in Chapter 3. Data analysis takes needs assessment or data gathering one step further. Data analysis provides the crucial linkage between data examination and the development of effective strategies. In this process the school planning committee interprets probable causal factors. These factors can be anything from a high dropout rate to a low attendance rate to low academic performance in specific curriculum areas.

In the simplest terms, this component of the Sorenson-Goldsmith Model is the "brain center" for the alignment of the school's delivery of instruction and related services to meet the needs of individual students. This component of the model also addresses knowledge management and the basic performance-related data and comparative data, as well as how such data is analyzed and used to optimize the school's performance.

Individual facts and isolated data do not typically provide an effective basis for establishing organizational priorities. This component of the model emphasizes the need for an alignment between analysis and school performance. This alignment ensures that analysis is relevant to decision making and that decision making is based on relevant data not statistical outliers or personal prejudices.

Collecting data without analyzing it is an exercise in futility. Data analysis can be a daunting task for the school planning committee particularly for the nonschool employee members as they face the "stack of stuff." This is where the school leader can provide the much-needed assistance and assurance, particularly to the nonschool committee members. The leader must ensure that acronyms and educational jargon are not freely thrown around by the committee educator members at the expense of the noneducator member's comprehension of the data. Educators may inadvertently speak in shorthand by saying things like, "LEP (Limited English Proficient), AYP (Adequate Yearly Progress), IDEA (Individuals With Disabilities Education Act), Title 1, or two deviations below the norm." Remember, this lingo is foreign to most of the nonschool committee members. The school leader must be sensitive to this issue and be certain the dialogue remains inclusive to all members of the committee.

Data must be disaggregated to obtain the level of specificity that is required to ensure that all students meet with success. Desegregation

Table 4.1   Ft. Chadbourne Elementary School State Academic
                 Performance Report

Fifth-Grade Mathematics

5th Math	State	Campus	Anglo	Hispanic	Black	Low SES	Male	Female
				% Passing				
This year	88	87	94	81	78	68	91	85
Last year	84	86	94	77	69	57	87	81

of data requires data to be differentiated by subpopulations. Examples of subpopulations include race, gender, and economic status.

One example of data desegregation is found in student achievement data. To better illustrate desegregation of student data we will examine an abridged report on student achievement in fifth-grade mathematics at the fictitious Ft. Chadbourne Elementary School (FCES) identified in Table 4.1.

In reviewing these data there are several observations that can be made about the mathematics results of students at Ft. Chadbourne Elementary School. The low SES score refers to students who are of low socioeconomic status. Low socioeconomic status is typically defined as being eligible to participate in the federal free or reduced lunch program.

Before reading the following list of authors' observations about FCES, stop and construct your own mental or physical list of observations based on your data analysis of the FCES performance report in Table 4.1. Compare the findings of your data analysis with that of the authors' 12 observations.

- The campus performed above state average last year and below state average this year.
- The Anglo subpopulation performed the highest in both years.
- The Hispanic subpopulation performed second highest in both years.
- The Hispanic subpopulation increased is performance by four points in the current year.
- The Black subpopulation performed the lowest of the three subpopulations both years.
- The Black population had the greatest increase in performance (nine points) of the three ethnic groups.
- The gap in achievement between the three ethnic groups is narrowing.

- The lowest performing subpopulation of any is the low SES group.
- Students who were in the low SES group made the greatest gains of any subpopulation.
- Males outperformed females each year.
- Males and females each improved their performance by four points.
- The profile of the most at-risk student at FCE based on these data is a Black female student who is on free or reduced lunch.

Hopefully after this brief analysis of the abridged data, other questions are forming about FCES, questions that will require additional data to be gathered by the collaborative planning committee.

What additional questions would provide a better understanding of the issues at FCES based on the data? Stop and develop your own list of questions about FCES that your initial data generated in your mind. A partial list of questions that might come to a committee member's mind based on data presented in Table 4.1 is listed below.

- What if any intervention was initiated that improved the performance of the Hispanic, Black, and Low SES subpopulations?
- What was the performance of these same groups of students on the tested mathematics objectives?
- Did the students perform poorly on the same math objectives each year?
- How did the students at the lower grades perform on mathematics in comparison to the fifth-grade students?
- Are there problems on the same type of objectives between the grade levels?
- How did this same group of students perform on the mathematics exam last year?
- Is the FCES mathematics curriculum aligned with the concepts assessed on the state exam?
- Do the same subpopulations have the lowest scores in other areas of the exam?
- What interventions were in last year's FCES school improvement plan? How effective were they?

This initial examination of the snippet of gathered data in Table 4.1 led to some obvious observations, which in turn, led to a greater depth of questioning and a need for assimilating additional data. (This requires the committee to revisit Component 3—Needs Assessment.) The analysis also led to the previous year's school plan and into the arena of school plan evaluation.

Had it been feasible to make the FCES example include more data than just that of student performance on mathematics at one grade level over a two-year period, more questions would have been generated. With a broader array of data, a broader field of needs would be identified. Earl and Katz (2005) call to our attention that, "Data do not provide right answers or quick fixes, but data offer decision-makers an opportunity to view a phenomenon through a number of different lenses to put forward hypotheses to challenge beliefs, and to pose more questions" (p. 19). This leads us to the fifth component of the Sorenson-Goldsmith Integrated Budget Model.

Component 5: Needs Prioritization

After completing the data-driven process of identifying the needs of the school, the school planning committee is frequently confronted with more needs than can be realistically addressed within the confines of both human and fiscal resources. At this point the committee must determine which of the needs should receive priority. Hopkins and West (1994) note that successful schools prioritize their needs and develop a few at a time.

A review of the data is an integral part in prioritizing the needs. Failure to use data knowledge can be costly to schools (Yeagley, 2002). Committee members must review the data at hand and reach consensus on what needs should receive top priority in order to propel the school toward the fulfillment of its mission. Fullan and Miles (1992) report that a cross-role group (i.e., school planning committee), a term they use to define a group with a variety of stakeholders, can assist in change. They observed, "different worlds collide, more learning occurs, and change is realistically managed" (Fullan & Miles, 1992, p. 752).

Conflict can arise while attempting to re-allocate resources. When needs have been identified using a data-driven process, the identified needs immediately possess a stronger status than those needs identified from a purely partisan process.

Prioritizing limited resources for data-driven needs is no doubt a challenge for all involved. The school leader must approach the situation in a nonpartisan manner. This is a situation where those skills and attributes embedded in ELCC/ISLLC Standard 5 are so important.

In our discussion of this standard in Chapter 3 we examined fairness—to be free from bias, dishonesty, or injustice. Fairness necessitates that we model to the planning team how to put the interests and needs of others above our own needs. It also requires us to remember that to best meet the needs of our students does not necessarily translate into equal distribution of the resources. We will need to allocate ample time for all to be heard and try to reach consensus. If the planning team approaches the situation with this mindset then the chances dramatically increase for a successful resolution that can be supported by the majority.

But what if resolution cannot be achieved? Then the leader must make a decision. This should be done with great caution for it has the potential to cause stakeholders to feel they really have no voice in the process and will become disenfranchised. If the situation is particularly sensitive, the planning committee should consider bringing in a knowledgeable neutral party who possesses conflict resolution skills to help them overcome their impasse. In the end, the process could draw the planning team closer together emotionally as well as missionally.

Component 6: Goal Setting

Goal setting is a crucial component in the integrated budget model. Goals can unify the stakeholders by providing them with meaning and purpose. Goals are broad statements of expected outcomes that are consistent with the mission, vision, and philosophy of the school. Goals should be driven by student-performance-based needs and should be consistent with the school's vision and mission statements (Oliva, 2005).

We must be sensitive when we begin in earnest to develop data-driven goals. Data can reveal differences in performance. It can point its digital finger to strengths and weaknesses in the school. This can make some stakeholders uneasy. The collaborative committee process cannot ignore where the data are pointing nor can it bury the facts. Academic integrity demands that the committee examine the actions dictated by the data and develop the appropriate goals.

The school planning committee must be involved in the goal-setting process because goals reflect the essence of the school's culture. When goals are assimilated into the school's culture, stakeholders are more motivated to achieve them and more likely to punish members who abandon them. In fact, goals can be so incorporated into the school's culture that they can continue to exist through changes of administration (Gorton, Schneider, & Fisher, 1988). Maeroff (1994) asserted that results-driven goals motivate and engage effective teams. It is imperative that the collaborative planning committee aids all of the stakeholders in making the connection between goals and improvement if there is to be a significant chance for improving the school.

The planning committee has gathered data, analyzed data, and prioritized needs. By this time in the planning process, each member of the committee should have a good understanding of why things are the way they are at the school. Ubben, Hughes, and Norris (2004) provide four assumptions to guide a principal in working with the school planning committee on goal setting. They are:

1. People at the working level tend to know the problems best.

2. The face-to-face work group is the best unit for diagnosis and change.

3. People will work hard to achieve objectives and goals they have helped develop.

4. Initiative and creativity are widely distributed in the population.

It is the responsibility of the school leader to keep the goals in front of the stakeholders. Goals should be distributed and displayed in a variety of forums such as PTA/PTO meetings and community service organization meetings. A goal should be reviewed at every faculty meeting, every grade level, or every department meeting. They should appear in faculty newsletters or emails; they should be posted on the school's website. They should be embedded in parent communications. Leithwood (1990), in describing goals wrote, " The glue that holds together the myriad actions and decisions of highly effective principals . . . [are] the goals that they and their staff [school planning committee] have developed for the school and a sense of what their schools need to look like and to do in order to accomplish those goals" (p. 85).

Component 7: Performance Objectives

Once goals congruent with the school's vision and mission have been established through the collaborative planning process, then performance-based objectives must be developed to provide increased definition to the course of action. Performance objectives identify specific, measurable and expected outcomes for all student populations served. Performance objectives should be driven by student performance-based needs assessment data. Table 4.2 contains two objectives. The first objective is not a performance objective. The second objective is a performance objective.

The first objective is not measurable because the students are being asked to do "well" in mathematics this year. "Well" is a subjective term and can vary from individual to individual in definition.

Table 4.2   A Comparison of a Nonperformance Objective to a
Performance Objective

Nonperformance Objective	Students will do well in mathematics this school year.
Performance Objective	Students scores in the state assessment exam on mathematics will increase by 5% in each of the ethnic subpopulations with an N>30.

This objective is also vague in that it not only lacks specificity, it does not prescribe a method for completing the measurement.

The second objective is a performance objective for three reasons: (1) a data source for the assessment is identified—the state assessment exam; (2) a specific improvement of 5% is expected in each of the ethnic subpopulations; and (3) it adds specific accountability to subpopulations.

It is essential that all objectives in the school action plan be measurable if the school is to be data-driven in its planning. When objectives are nonmeasurable, it is left up to each individual to employ personal feelings on whether the objective has been achieved. Ten different individuals could evaluate the objective ten different ways.

Component 8: Action Plan

The action plan is the *living* document that serves as a guide for all of the stakeholders. Emphasis was added to the adjective living to call attention to the fact that the action plan is not static. (If it's static, it's likely to be dead.) The action plan is a living, breathing document. This point cannot be overemphasized. A quick review of the Sorenson-Goldsmith Model in Figure 4.1 reminds us that much effort is required to produce this meaningful document. The process began by defining and selecting the stakeholders to create the school planning committee. Gathering and analyzing data from a plethora of sources followed the creation of this committee. Next, needs prioritization allowed for the identification of the actions essential for the school to fulfill its mission. Goals and objectives were then put in place to create a step-by-step blueprint to turn the prioritized needs into prioritized fulfillments.

This entire process is chronicled in the action plan where greater detail is added by including strategies and actions. But the process does not stop when the plan is put in writing or posted online. This is just the beginning of the action plan's function. At the base of the model in Figure 4.1 is a box with three terms—ongoing evaluation, analysis, and course correction. This foundational concept of the model demands that the action plan be a breathing document. Ongoing means that the process never ceases. Ongoing evaluation and analysis requires continuous monitoring. This action will manifest itself in ongoing course correction that will result in editing marks appearing throughout the action plan.

A Planning Metaphor

When you board a plane in New York to fly to Los Angeles, the pilot has already filed a flight plan with the proper authorities. Once the plane departs New York, the pilot, copilot, and navigator continually reference the flight plan to ensure that the plane and its passengers meet the goal of the flight—to arrive in Los Angeles with all the passengers and the plane in safe condition. Despite the effort of the plane's crew in submitting a viable flight plan that when implemented under static conditions would allow the flight crew, passengers, and plane to meet its goal, events will occur during the flight that will require the crew to make course corrections in the flight plan.

As the plane approaches Missouri, it encounters severe thunderstorms. The pilot and crew consult and agree upon modifications to the plan so as to circumvent this unexpected weather event. Later, as the plane is approaching Nevada, a passenger becomes seriously ill. After a quick needs assessment of the situation, the crew decides to make an emergency landing in Las Vegas to secure the appropriate medical treatment for this passenger.

The plane leaves Las Vegas to finish the flight to LAX. Unfortunately, air traffic was stacked up and the plane was diverted to a holding pattern until space was available. After 45 minutes of circling Los Angeles, the plane makes a safe landing. The flight plan, along with the course corrections initiated by the flight crew, allowed everyone to celebrate the success of the plan by experiencing a safe arrival. But what about the passenger who was left in Las Vegas, you might ask. This passenger received the appropriate medical treatment. The airline then gave the passenger a ticket from Las Vegas to Los Angeles so he could reach his final destination. Granted, he did not reach it at the same time as the others. But through the appropriate accommodations, he achieved the goal of the original flight plan.

There are several similarities between this flight and a school year. Like the flight crew, the school planning committee creates and files a flight plan, but it is called a school action plan. The plane's flight is representative of the implementation of the flight plan. Likewise, the school's activities during the school year represent the implementation of the school action plan. Both the plane and the school will encounter unanticipated events that will require its crews to revisit the original plan and incorporate the necessary changes to keep the plane or school on course to meet their goals. Failure to understand that no action plan is ever written that does not require constant monitoring and adjustments will doom the flight or the school to failure.

This constant monitoring and implementation of change is represented two ways on the integrated budget model in Figure 4.1. First it is represented by a pair of double-pointed arrows above the ongoing evaluation, analysis, and course correction box at the base of the model. These arrows illustrate the need for constant monitoring of the action plan. Likewise, constant monitoring is symbolized by the quad arrow at the center of the model. Constant monitoring and adjusting is at the center of the model's effectiveness. Visualize the quad arrow rotating while moving along a horizontal axis between the eight components. This visualization reminds us that the planning process must not only be constantly monitored but that it is also not a linear process.

Planning may progress from Component 1 through Component 8, but in the monitoring process the committee can return to whatever component is necessary to make the appropriate course correction. For example, new data might be gathered (Component 3) which will be analyzed (Component 4) which will then necessitate action in Components 7 and 8.

This is exactly what happened in the New York to Los Angeles flight. The flight crew analyzed new data—a weather report. This analysis caused the crew to modify the flight plan to meet the goal of a safe flight. As school leaders, we must ensure that our flight plans, which in reality are our action plans, are constantly monitored and appropriately adjusted.

The Elements of an Action Plan

It is time to construct a flight—that is—an action plan. The process begins with an overview of the elements of a school action plan:

- Coversheet
- List of SBDM committee members
- School vision and mission statements
- School goals (if a campus plan, district goals should also be in place and cross referenced where applicable)
- One action plan strategy page for each strategy

The coversheet design is an individual school's choice, as is the design of the listing of the school planning committee members and the vision and mission statements. It is important to include the vision and mission statements to keep them in front of all of the school's stakeholders since they are at the core of the school's culture and climate. People are busy and are bombarded with information. Including these statements makes it convenient for the stakeholders to refresh their memories on these important statements.

The GOSA Relationship

Goals, objectives, strategies, and actions bring structure and detail to the planning process. These facets of planning are integrated on the action strategy pages in the school action plan. Understanding the relationship between these four planning facets is essential to understanding the school action plan. This relationship is illustrated in Figure 4.2.

Goals, the G in GOSA, were examined earlier in Component 6 of the Sorenson-Goldsmith Model. Measurable objectives, the O in GOSA, were explained in the discussion of Component 7 of the model.

The S in GOSA is strategy. A strategy is a statement that assigns resources to accomplish the goal and objective that it supports. Examples of resources include but are not limited to fiscal, information, employee, material, spatial, and technology.

Strategies can be broad initiatives that cover the breadth of a school. Examples include a math-manipulative program, a new tutorial design, or a dropout prevention intervention. The strategy should be expected to significantly impact the performance of the targeted populations.

Figure 4.2   The GOSA Relationship

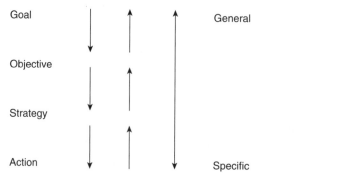

An example of a strategy statement is: Implement a computerized reading lab that targets students who are reading one or more grade levels below their grade placement.

The A in GOSA is activity—a particular action that is required to implement a strategy. An example of an activity to be used in the strategy is: The director of technology will order 20 computers according to bid specifications.

Reading the GOSA elements in Figure 4.2 from the top to the bottom increases the specificity. The opposite occurs when they are read from the bottom to the top. The elements become more general. This unique relationship allows the document to be examined on four different levels of detail. Reading only the goals and objectives provides the reader with a quick general understanding of the school action plan. Reading all four levels provides the reader with the detail required for implementation of the goals and objectives.

An Example

Figure 4.3 is a completed strategy page from a school action plan. There is one goal on the page—All students will master the objectives of the mathematics curriculum. The goal is a broad statement supporting the school's mission of academic success for all students. It is also linked to student performance-based needs.

The objective is specific and measurable. It focuses on the mathematics goal and uses the results of the state assessment examination as its measure of mastery. Greater accountability is further achieved in that the objective is calling for a 5% increase in the performance of all identified student subpopulations.

The strategy, using the *Math Ace It* software program, assigns resources to support the goal and objective. Greater specificity of who, what, when, and where is provided with the inclusion of six specific action statements. For example, responsibilities are assigned to the principal, counselor, lab supervisor, and lead teacher. An accountability system is also in place for both formative and summative evaluation. The location of the evaluation data is even specified.

Finally, on this strategy page from a campus action plan, the integration of the budget with the vision and planning process is clearly in evidence (see Figure 4.3). Fiscal resources were budgeted as evidenced by $8,500 in funds being assigned to this strategy as well as personnel resources and facility resources. The allocated resources supported the school's vision of having all students master the mathematics curriculum. Planning is evidenced in the campus action plan through the strategy pages and minutes of the planning committee.

Figure 4.3   Strategy Page from the Ft. Chadbourne Elementary School Campus Action Plan

Goal 1: All students will master the objectives of the mathematics curriculum.

Objective 1: Student mastery of the mathematics curriculum as measured by the state assessment exam will increase by 5% or more in each identified subpopulation.

Strategy 1: Students will use a diagnostic and instructionally managed *Math Ace It* software program to remediate specific mathematics objectives they are having difficulty in mastering.

Actions	Responsibility	Timeline (Start/End)	Resources (Human Material Fiscal)	Audit (Formative)	Reported Documented
1. Purchase *Math Ace It* software.	Principal	May 05/ July 05	$ 7, 000	Purchase order	Principal's office
2. Provide faculty training on *Math Ace It* software.	Principal	August 05	Consultant, $ 1500	Purchase order agenda	Principal's office
3. Provide math teachers with a list of identified students based on state assessment scores.	Counselor	August 05	Counselor	Student lists	Counselor's office
4. Assign students to three 30-minute sessions per week in the computer lab.	Lab supervisor	August 05/ Ongoing	Lab supervisor	Student lists	Computer lab
5. Provide teachers with progress reports on students.	Lab supervisor	2nd & 4th Fridays	Lab supervisor	Progress reports	Teacher files
6. Monthly planning meetings with the principal.	Lead teacher	4th Friday	Teachers	Agenda/ minutes	Lead Teacher

Evaluation (Summative): State Assessment reports, *Math Ace It* Reports

Table 4.3   Integration of Vision, Planning, and Budget in the
Ft. Chadbourne Elementary School

Strategy Page	
Budget	$8,500, personnel assigned, facility space assigned
Vision	Seeking mastery of mathematics by all students
Planning	Use of a planning team, page from the campus action plan

GOSA Mapping

The school action plan is actually the integration and coordination of multiple GOSA relationships that are designed to fulfill the school planning committee's identified and prioritized school needs. A truncated illustration of this integrated GOSA design embedded in the school action plan is provided in Figure 4.4. This is, in essence, a graphic depiction of the school action plan. How many action plan strategy pages would be used in the plan in Figure 4.4? If you said 14 you are correct. Count the strategies across the figure and you will come up with 14.

Figure 4.4   GOSA Relationships Map

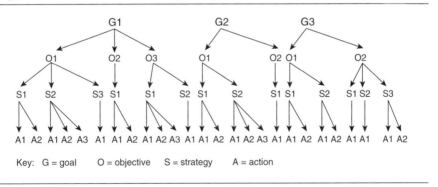

Key: G = goal   O = objective   S = strategy   A = action

Final Thoughts

The principles of this book cannot be implemented overnight. It will require a significant amount of commitment and labor, but students will reap benefits in the long run. The transition to an integrated budget-vision-planning process evolves through four stages. (See Figure 4.5.) The first stage, the Reactive Stage is characterized by poorly defined goals and random strategies, and activities designed to meet immediate needs. There is no coordination between the three factors, since they are headed in completely different directions. The second stage is the Transitive Stage. In this stage there is evidence of a beginning of the alignment of goals, objectives, and strategies. Vision, planning, and budget are pointed in the same general directions. There are still deficiencies in planning and coordinating between the three elements. In the third stage, the Aligned Stage, alignment has been achieved between the budget, planning, and vision process, but there is not integration among all elements. The final stage is the Integrated Stage. By this time, an amalgam has been created using vision, planning, and

Figure 4.5   The Four Stages of the Implementation of the Sorenson-
                   Goldsmith Integrated Budget Model

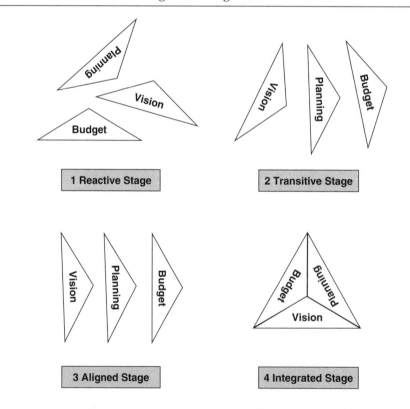

budget. Collaboration and communication are now valued. Continuous evaluation and course correction is in place. The three elements are now one. They are all aiming toward the center pointing toward success.

Schools need all stakeholders working together to ensure academic success for everyone. No family wants their child to be the student who does not meet with academic success. The construction of a school action plan that integrates the school's vision with its budget greatly increases the likelihood of achieving the school's vision and mission.

It is up to the school leaders to keep the vision and the plan in front of the stakeholders. Remember, like the flight from New York to Los Angeles, your school year will have situations that will require the school planning team to revisit the school action plan and make the necessary course adjustments throughout the school year. In the end, if everyone works collaboratively and commits to a well-constructed and managed plan, success happens.

P.S.

Odden and Archibald (2001) remind us that the "reform goal is rarely accompanied by a 'fiscal note' which is legislative lingo for identifying the cost of achieving such a goal" (p. 2). We will never have enough resources to do everything we want to do for our students. The integrated budget model provides us with an opportunity to rearrange our resources and use them in a more efficient manner. When we stop and think about it, this is in reality an *increase* in revenue without asking more from the taxpayers.

Discussion Questions

1. What are the advantages of having procedures and polices in place to define the roles and responsibilities of the school planning committee?

2. What are the advantages of providing training to school planning committee members?

3. Describe four attributes of a data-driven school?

4. Data Analysis, the fourth component of the Sorenson-Goldsmith School Budgeting-Vision Implementation Model

was referenced as the "brain center": of this model. What is the significance of this nickname for the fourth component of this model?

5. How is the quote at the beginning of the chapter relevant to the topics of this chapter?

6. How could you re-write this nonmeasurable objective into a measurable objective? "More students will take AP courses next year."

7. How does the Fullan and Miles quote, "different worlds collide, more learning occurs, and change is realistically managed" manifest itself in the needs prioritization step of the process?

Case Study Application: Shifting Paradigms With Changing Times

Note: This case study is designed to lead the reader through the Sorenson-Goldsmith Integrated Budget Model. In order to assist the reader in obtaining a global view of how this model functions, parts of the process are provided. The budget amounts are unrealistic but were kept small so the reader does not become bogged down in mathematics. Frequent references to Figure 4.1 can assist in observing the flow of the model through this case study.

Part 1 The Deal: Components 1 and 2 of the Integrated Budget Model

The Situation

Waterview is a prosperous suburb on Pecan Bay just south of the thriving seaport of Indianola. With a population of 25,000, Waterview has grown in the last 25 years from a sleepy coastal village to a thriving community where new industries and businesses continue to locate. Waterview is the county seat of Fannin County; it also meets the educational needs of the entire county. Fannin Consolidated School District (FCSD) has two high schools, four middle schools, and ten elementary schools. While the county's population has continued to decline for the past 20 years, Waterview is an exception. As a result of the population growth, two new middle schools and four new elementary schools have been built in Waterview in the past decade.

Two years ago, Dr. Ronald Scotts was named superintendent of FCSD. Dr. Scotts, a 48-year-old father of 13-year-old twin girls, moved with his wife Juanita from the upstate town of River City. While serving as the associate superintendent for finance, Dr. Scotts earned a reputation in River City as a strong and competent leader particularly in school finance and personnel. The FCSD board hired Dr. Scotts to bring about change to the school system. Academic performance for the last 10 years was consistently mediocre. Routines had become the norm. The last innovation in the district was 10 years ago, and it was an automated substitute-teacher assignment system. The board with its three newly elected members wants FCSD to move from an attitude of mediocrity to one of excellence.

During his first year as superintendent, Dr. Scotts started a dialogue with the administrators about a decentralization plan for the school district. At the end of this year, before the principals started taking their vacations, Dr. Scotts announced that in the fall he would provide an allocation of $10,000 to schools that wanted to receive training in a collaborative planning process. Principals would need to submit a plan outlining how the funding would be spent to train the faculty in the collaborative planning process. Dr. Scotts further told the principals that campuses with an operational campus planning committee would assume responsibility for the development, spending, and monitoring of the campus budget with the exception of salaries and maintenance and operations. With this newfound autonomy came accountability for the effective use of the budgeted funds.

Dr. Hector Avila and Ms. Abigail Grayson are in their second year at Pecan Bay High School. Dr. Avila had previously been a middle school principal in an urban district before being named principal at PBHS. He is the first Hispanic principal in the district. He has been well received by the community. Dr. Avila was hired to be a change agent at PBHS. Dr. Avila has the gift of being able to unite people behind a shared vision. Ms. Grayson had taught mathematics and had been the girls' basketball and softball coach at PBHS for the past five years. Ms. Grayson has a much-deserved reputation as an innovative classroom teacher who is willing to try new teaching strategies. Ms. Grayson attended mathematics training at a local university through a Teacher Quality Grant during the past two summers. Hector and Abigail like each other, and each one's talents complement the other's.

After Dr. Scotts concluded his $10,000 challenge, Hector and Abigail immediately and aggressively spent two weeks on campus writing a proposal that was well documented by research and contained a detailed implementation plan based on the Sorenson-Goldsmith Integrated Budget Model. The two delivered the plan in person to Dr. Scotts to demonstrate their enthusiasm for the project. Dr. Scotts inwardly smiled and thanked the two for the proposal. Two weeks later Pecan Bay High School became the first campus in FCSD to have its collaborative planning proposal approved.

During the first day of staff development in late summer, Abigail and Hector excitedly explained to the faculty their proposal using a PowerPoint presentation with coordinated handouts. The faculty was quiet. The principals were picking up on the body language that they were "bombing." Finally, Ed Feeney, a veteran teacher of 27 years at PBHS broke the passive silence and asked, "Whose idea was this? Sounds like the superintendent wants us to do his work. I'm busy enough as it is." There was some applause. Latasha Jackson, a fourth-year drama teacher asked, "Is this another one of those fads that goes through schools? I bet the state is up to this." Kelly Tyres, a paraprofessional commented, "No one ever asks us what we want. They just keep shoving stuff down our throat like the 'highly qualified' stuff from NCLB."

The two principals let the teachers go to lunch 30 minutes early (very popular) and went back to their offices, surprised and beaten. They kept repeatedly saying things to each other like, "Where did we go wrong?" and "I can't believe they are so negative," and "Where do we go from here?"

Thinking It Through

Hector and Abigail desperately need your assistance. Where did they go wrong? Where do they go from here? Hector and Abigail have a great proposal and are very capable administrators; yet they encountered strong resistance from the faculty. As that "other set of eyes," you need to stop at this point in the case study and write a step-by-step plan for these principals to win over the faculty. Some *Handy Hints* have been included to help you with this process.

You will discover that if you do this activity with several colleagues your intervention plan will be stronger than if you complete it by yourself.

Handy Hints

- Involve all stakeholders
- Talk mission and vision
- Communication
- Shared decision making
- Identify challenges
- Identify strengths
- Outside resources

Part 2 The Needs: Components 3–5 of the Sorenson-Goldsmith Integrated Budget Model

Checking It Out

Thank you for your assistance in developing a step-by-step plan for assisting the PBHS faculty to reconsider and adopt the collaborative planning process! Your work is not done. Learning to use the collaborative process requires time and effort by all the stakeholders in a school. Read on and be prepared to provide assistance again as the process continues to unfold.

With the arrival of spring, the campus planning committee was established and the training completed. It is time to begin constructing PBHS's first ever campus-based action plan with an integrated budget. The campus planning committee has been provided a packet of data courtesy of Dr. Avila and Ms. Grayson. The data was gathered from a variety of sources. The principals spent countless hours in gathering this data but only did so as a way to assist and encourage the committee in its inaugural year. The committee is free to gather any other data as it sees fit. The two principals have volunteered to assist the committee in data gathering. Dr. Scotts was pleased to inform the campus planning committee that PBHS would receive an allotment of $100,000 for the next school year. Nelson Clampett, the assistant superintendent of finance, has trained the appropriate individuals on the district's budgeting software. Nelson is anxious to see his old alma mater meet with success. In fact it was 17 years ago that he led the Fighting Squirrels baseball team to the state championship by pitching a no hitter in the state championship game. Since that time, the school has not received any athletic or academic award.

In order to assist the flow of this case study, the planning committee's work of data gathering and analysis (Components 3 and 4) has been completed for you. The committee spent several meetings analyzing the box of data provided by the principals. They requested additional data and were provided with all the data they requested.

Make a list of data that you would want to have if you were on the Fighting Squirrels campus planning team.

Thinking It Through

It is now time to proceed to Component 5 of the Sorenson-Goldsmith Integrated Budget Model. You must take the nonprioritized list of 10 identified needs by the PBHS planning committee and prioritize them. Remember PBHS has an allocation of $100,000. The committee cannot exceed the budget allocation! Note that the identified needs will cost substantially more than the campus's allocation. It is time for the committee to make some tough decisions. Assign your priority numbers to the needs using the column on the far left. Provide a written rationale to share with the faculty and administration to defend your needs prioritization.

Table 4.4   PBHS Nonprioritized Identified Needs

Next Year

Your Priority	*Cost*	*Identified NEED*	*Committee Rationale*
	$10,000	Copier contract	Used by all departments Basis of many academic assignments
	$15,000	Reading intervention plan $12,000 for software $3,000 for training	% Freshmen reading below grade level is twice the state rate % Hispanics reading below grade level is three times the state rate Teacher survey shows reading issues number one on teacher concerns
	$20,000	General supplies	Meet basic office/classroom needs of paper, staplers, tape, etc.

(Continued)

Table 4.4 (Continued)

Next Year

Your Priority	Cost	Identified NEED	Committee Rationale
	$3,000	Special Olympics	Add this program since these students are unable to participate in other extracurricular events Parent advocacy group has made an appeal to the SBDM committee
	$15,000	New band uniforms	Current uniforms are 23 years old Uniforms were water damaged and now have a mold problem
	$6,000	Graphing calculators	Needed in advanced science and math classes. Essential to meet state curriculum requirements Needed in Pre-AP, AP, and dual credit courses
	$5,000	Professional travel	New category Teachers need to be able to expand their knowledge by attending Number 4 need on the teacher survey
	$30,000	Expanded technology in the library and computer center $15,000 tech services $10,000 printers $5,000 supplies	Students need access to Internet and other technology for AP, dual credit courses, research Identified by teachers of advanced courses as a number one priority

Your Priority	*Cost*	*Identified NEED*	*Committee Rationale*
	$30,000	9th-grade school-within-a-school $5,000 training $15,000 facility upgrades $10,000 curriculum materials	High failure rate in freshmen classes High referral rate to office High absentee rate
	$7,000	Spring athletic banquet $5,000 honorarium for speaker $2,000 catered meals for 200	Boost enthusiasm for athletics Increase school spirit

Part 3 The Action Plan: Components 6–8 of the Sorsenson-Goldsmith Integrated Budget Model

Now that you have prioritized the needs it is time to construct an *abridged* action plan. For the purpose of this case study, you will only use the top two prioritized needs. As you proceed through this portion of the case study it might be helpful to review the figures in Chapter 4 as well as the information in components six through eight.

Using the number one prioritized need, complete a strategy page to address the prioritized need. It may be necessary to use more than one strategy page due to space constraints. A clean copy of the strategy page is located in Resource A.

Repeat the process for the need you designated as the second priority. Once you have completed both priorities review your pages. Are the goals, objectives, and strategies aligned and logical? Do the actions clearly define what was being done in order to implement the strategy? Are the resources, personnel, and evaluations in place?

Using your strategy pages, construct a GOSA map for your abridged action plan. Use the following scaffolding items to assist you in the construction of your GOSA map.

- How many different **g**oals did you have? _____ (Probably 1 or 2)
- How many different **o**bjectives did you have? _____ (Probably 1 or 2)
- How many **s**trategies did you have? _____ (Probably less than 5)
- How many **a**ctions did you have? _____ (Probably many more than the number of strategies.
- Review your GOSA map. Does it contain the same number of the different elements that you identified in the previous questions? If so that is a strong indication that your mapping is on the right track.
- Using your strategy pages and your GOSA map, compare your actions to the strategies on the strategy pages to their counterpart on the map. Do they connect on the map as they do on the strategy pages? Repeat the process for the strategy-objective relationship and the objective-goal relationship. If they are aligned, this, along with a yes answer to the previous questions, indicates that you have successfully completed this final portion of the case study.

5

Effective and Efficient Budgeting Practices

I find all this money a considerable burden!

—J. Paul Getty

The Budget Plan

While J. Paul Getty no doubt found his extensive personal wealth to be a "considerable burden," it is not our wish nor our intention, for the school budgeting process to be nearly as complicated or problematic for the educational leader. In fact, our greatest desire is for the school administrator, as the budget manager, to find the practice of school budgeting to be both efficient and effective. With this thought in mind, let's turn to the first rule of school budgeting: The secret of successful budgeting is three-part: visionary manifestation, constancy in planning, and interminable linkage to school goals and objectives.

Theoretically, and most certainly appropriate in practice, the school academic or action plan should be developed in tandem with the budget plan which serves to identify the costs necessary to support the academic plan and instructional program. The budget plan is then converted into fund-oriented accounts (a school budget) as associated with the monetary allotment provided to the school by the local district. The rationale for such planning only makes sense because the obligation of any school administrator is to—first and foremost—plan for the specified needs of the students and not permit the available funds to "be the master or limiting factor in determining the bounds of the educational program" (Brimley & Garfield, 2005, p. 306). Unfortunately, all too often, a lack of integrated budget and academic planning at the school or district level results in the selection and application of programs and services that are short-sighted, insufficient, and ineffective in meeting the varied needs of the students served—resulting in wasted revenue and poor academic performance.

The purpose of the budget plan is to support the school action plan and consolidate it into dollar appropriations. Basically, any academic or action plan is worth nothing more than the paper it is written on unless it is integrated with the budget plan. Table 5.1 specifies the necessary steps that a school administrator and decision-making team should follow in relation to the budgetary process which includes training, planning, and development.

The budget plan must be developed with the following questions in mind:

1. Prior to any budget planning and development process, has the school leader provided the necessary professional development training that is essential to understanding how vision and

Table 5.1 The Budgetary Process — Training, Planning, and Development

1	2	3	4	5	6	7
Professional Development	Vision-Making and Needs Assessment	Goal Development	Programmatic Identification and Development	Budget Plan Development	Budget Implementation	Budget Monitoring and Evaluation

8
◀ Has the learning community been actively involved? ▶

The budgetary process from training to planning to actual development is a constant course of action that requires a school leader to engage the decision-making team in a collaborative and problem-solving effort. This table illustrates how the school leader can transform the budgetary process into a step-by-step dimension that clarifies the complexities often associated with budget development, specifically as it correlates with vision-making and goal-setting. This constant evolving and ever-revolving process allows for a continuous commitment to instructional and programmatic change, and further provides for all parties involved to actively and constructively engage in a budgetary process that promotes ongoing assessment, design, planning, development, feedback, integration, implementation, and evaluation. Dealing with the visionary aspect of planning and the analytical considerations associated with budgeting can be a source of intellectual pleasure and growth, for both the decision-making team and the budget manager.

planning impact programmatic considerations and the school budget?

2. Has a needs assessment been conducted to address what impact does programmatic initiatives—such as federal, state, and local—have on student achievement? (See the subsequent section on Adequate Funding in an Era of Accountability.) Levin (1991) suggests that school leaders want to know which particular interventions are most promising for increasing student achievement and cost the least because monetary resources are often in short supply. He further notes that "it is important to maximize the effectiveness of those resources, and this can be done by using strategies that promise the largest amount of effectiveness per unit of cost" (p. 192). This is what a needs assessment is all about.

3. Have student needs and academic achievement been addressed in the form of a school action plan that emphasizes goal development?

4. Following the needs assessment and goal development, have specific instructional as well as nonacademic programs been identified for improvement or exclusion?

5. Have learning community representatives been provided with forms and figures that are indicative of previous budgetary allotments and expenditures for at least one prior year?

6. Has the learning community (specifically the teaching staff) been asked by school administration to submit requests for supplies, equipment, and facilities that are essential, if not critical, in meeting the academic needs of the students served and are further necessary in relation to the dictates imposed on the school or district academic programs by state and federal mandates?

7. Have budgeted dollars been allocated to support the action plan, and has the budget manager and team regularly monitored and evaluated budgetary expenditures in relation to programmatic effectiveness and student academic gains? This is more than a "wish list" approach to instruction and school budgeting—this is an integrated-visionary process, through a needs-assessment approach, that readily identifies priorities which are necessary for programmatic success.

8. Finally, have faculty, staff, students, parents, and community members been actively involved in the decision-making process leading to the development of the school action plan and budget?

Each of these eight components represents sound budgeting theory which better serves to ensure that the ideas and recommendations of the learning community are actively sought and incorporated into the budgetary process.

Adequate Funding in an Era of Accountability

Recent education policy efforts at both the national and state level have focused on standards-based reforms and assessments that place greater responsibility on school districts and, most notably, on site leaders to effect school change and improvement. Accountability mandates focus on aligning curriculum and assessments to rigorous academic standards, using high-stakes testing. This movement is at the center of most state and federal accountability mandates (O'Shea, 2005). The federal No Child Left Behind Act (NCLB) of 2001 is most reflective of such policy initiatives and moreover mandates that all teachers be of high quality, identifies schools in need of assistance, and, furthermore, provides educational options for students attending Title I schools that do not make adequate progress for two consecutive years. Each of these dictates, central to NCLB, cost money—money that school districts often do not have.

Current funding systems have yet to adequately "link the availability of funds and the educational performance of students" (Reschovsky & Imazeki, 2000, p. 1). To date, while several strategies have been examined, necessary funding has been limited in meeting the implementation efforts necessary to fulfill the federal guidelines associated with NCLB (Sergiovanni, et al., 2004). While states and districts are continually attempting to evaluate how school sites are utilizing their funding resources to improve student outcomes, much work remains to be done to adequately ensure that school expenditures equate to school improvements. As a result, school leaders must continually contemplate and address the challenge of making every budgeted dollar stretch to meet mandated instructional initiatives, individual student needs, teacher requests, parent demands, district desires, and state expectations. No wonder a principal was recently heard to exclaim: "My budget is stretched so tight, it squeaks!"

Analyzing the School Action and Budget Plans

The school action plan, as previously examined in Chapter 4, serves as the vehicle that drives not only the instructional program but the budget development process as well. Effective budgetary planning must allow for the school budget to be based upon the educational programs designated within the confines of an action or improvement plan. In other words, funding should be allocated to the educational programs as identified in priority order in the school action plan. There are numerous aspects or designators often associated with an action plan. In the state of Texas, for example, there are 13 designations within an action plan as mandated by the Texas Education Agency (2005) which further comply with the No Child Left Behind Act (2001). These 13 designators are identified as: (1) student performance, (2) special education, (3) violence prevention, (4) parental involvement, (5) professional development, (6) suicide prevention, (7) conflict resolution, (8) dyslexia treatment programs, (9) dropout reduction, (10) technology, (11) discipline management, (12) accelerated instruction, and (13) career education. While each of these designators is mandated in one particular state, it is noteworthy to recognized that as a whole, they are quite representative of school planning issues that any state, district, or school might encounter.

Budget plans must be developed in tandem with an action or improvement plan. The budget plan serves effectively to (1) project all anticipated income, (2) identify all needed programs, and (3) project current and future average daily attendance or membership for the purpose of seeking a district allocation that will serve to meet the needs of all the students enrolled.

The purpose of the budget plan is to anticipate, project, and predict potential sources of income, program development, any financial deficit, and potential areas for budgetary reduction or additions. The development of the budget plan, much like that of the action plan, should be made in collaboration with the school-based decision-making team. This team, following the guidance of the school leader, is most often involved in decisions related to educational planning, curriculum development, instructional issues, staffing patterns, professional development, school organization, and of course, budgeting.

Prior to the process of developing the budget plan, the effective school administrator must insist and ensure that a professional development program has been initiated to train the learning community in the methods of generating and completing a needs assessment (see Table 5.2). Identified in Chapter 4 is a needs-assessment process (see Component 3 of the integrated budget model in Figure 4.1) that appropriately correlates with budget and action planning. When utilized appropriately, a needs-assessment instrument can do just what its name implies, and can further serve as the impetus for prioritizing

Table 5.2   Conducting a Needs Assessment

Phase	Work to Accomplish
I. Initiating the inquiry process. 1. What areas/aspects of the school program need improvement? 2. Why do we believe these areas/aspects need improvement? 3. What pertinent sources of data are available to verify any need improvement? 4. What other sources of data might be considered or needed? 5. How can we gather all the necessary data?	1. Review the district's and school's mission or visionary statement. 2. Identify pertinent available sources of data (e.g., campus action plan, previous studies, local and statewide test results, surveys of teachers, students, parents, follow-up studies of graduates, etc.). 3. Identify other needed sources of data that may not be readily available, and determine what methods or procedures are needed to collect any particular data.
II. Deriving consensus on the concerns/needs/problems to be addressed. 1. Can consensus be reached in terms of the areas/aspects of the school program that need improvement? 2. Are these areas/aspects of sufficient significance for substantive schoolwide improvement? 3. For which areas/aspects are sharp differences of opinion noted? 4. How were these differences resolved? 5. What sources of data were needed to help resolve any differences?	1. Review all pertinent sources of data. 2. Consider all concerns, problems, and needs that have been identified. 3. Consider any new or overlooked problems or needs. 4. Derive consensus and "narrow-down" the list of needs.
III. Developing and implementing the process of organizing and examining all pertinent data, and making a tentative determination of priority. 1. Which concerns/problems/needs are the most significant for improving the school's overall program?	1. Discuss each area of concern, problem, or need and outline specific actions to be implemented. 2. Be prepared to share action or implementation proposals with your clientele or constituency.

(Continued)

Table 5.2 (Continued)

Phase	Work to Accomplish
2. Which are within the school's scope and capability for effective action and implementation? 3. How do the data relate to each identified problem/need? 4. What do the data reveal?	
IV. Focusing on the concerns/ problems/needs of highest priority. 1. What priority should be given to each identified concern/problem/ need? 2. Priorities should be determined by the following criteria: • How significant is this priority and what are the prospects for effecting substantive school-wide improvement? • What human, fiscal, and/or material resources (including release time) are required? • Is there sufficient expertise available internally and/or externally? 3. Is there a sound research base in the professional literature for addressing each prioritized concern/problem/need, and for supporting the proposed actions and/or implementations?	1. Review the research literature. 2. Conduct a full examination or discussion regarding each proposal. 3. Present recommendations to the district administrative leader (superintendent or designee) the priority rankings of each need. 4. Most important—work together as a team in the most collaborative manner and reach a fair and equitable consensus.

SOURCE: D. Tanner and L. Tanner, *Curriculum Development: Theory Into Practice.* (Englewood Cliffs, NJ: Prentice-Hall, 1995)

school-based needs with students and the academic program in the forefront of any budgetary consideration.

Generated Income Sources

"If you can conceive it, you can achieve it!" Do you recall this old adage? School leaders are designated many responsibilities, the budgetary

process being obviously one, and as a result are often called upon to put such an adage to work. The effective school administrator must quickly learn to generate additional sources of income for the school beyond those funds already allocated by district administration. The district allocation is just one of numerous income sources that must be generated if a school is to establish a comprehensive, high quality, and cost-effective program (Herman & Herman, 2001).

Swanson and King (1997) report that tax limitation efforts in many states have threatened to reduce local revenue and as a result, school officials have increasingly sought nontraditional sources of funding for schools. Such nontraditional income sources often include grants from both governmental entities as well as private foundations, gifts from business (adopt-a-school) partnerships, from individuals within the community, and from various corporations who are most interested in maintaining their commitment to education and to educational organizations. Income from many of these sources can be generated locally when a school administrator and team actively seek to make contact with these potential contributors (Vail, 1998).

Grants

Grants, for example, often provide an additional source of income for schools but are typically obtained on a competitive basis. Grant funds are generally tied to a Request for Application (RFA) process whereby a great deal of time and effort, not to mention tedious research and data collection, must occur for an application to be seriously considered. Most grants are categorical in nature, as previously noted in Chapter 1. As a reminder, *categorical* refers to funds that are restricted to certain "categories" or activities such as technology, science, or mathematics, or accelerated instruction. These funds can only be utilized within the particular category in which they were awarded and must further be monitored and accounted for, and, just as important, the instructional program funded must be frequently evaluated, often by outside sources or agencies, to ensure that the grant dollars are appropriately allotted, utilized, and expended. Listed below are a number of important attributes associated with grant funding.

- Grants are generally time sensitive—funded dollars must be appropriated and spent within a specific period of time.
- Grants are generally available from state or federal agencies and are often related to certain educational acts or initiatives— NCLB, for example.

- Grants and funding information can be identified and located by accessing governmental, commercial, nonprofit, and educational organization Web sites or home pages. Two excellent resources for educators seeking grant funding are by Peterson (2001) and Brewer, et al. (2001).
- Grants are generally restrictive—"in-kind" funds, for example, may be required whereby the funding agency expects the school or district to match the granted allotment with either dollars or services—transportation, custodial, equipment, or facilities usage are typical examples. Often the granted funds are further restricted and may not be used for furniture or travel or in some cases, salaries, for example. Such restrictions must be adhered to, or a school or district risks losing the grant and thus the dollars badly needed.

One example of grant funding is the *Teacher Quality Enhancement* grant (http://www.ed.gov/offices/OPE/heatqp/). This NCLB-related grant program provides opportunities for faculty development in the area of math and science. Schools collaborate with universities and other entities to provide staff training in support of systematic change and development at a fraction of the cost to a school district in comparison to the cost associated with a district providing the training independent of the contributing entities.

A second example is the *Bilingual Professional Development Program* grant (http://www.ed.gov/offices/OBEMLA/fy2000.html). This grant provides funding to ensure that school personnel are well-prepared to provide services to limited English-proficient (LEP) students.

A third example is the *21st Century Community Learning Centers* grant (http://www.ed.gov/21stcclc/). This funding initiative aids with the formation of school-community partnerships to help keep local schools open after hours and during the summer.

Finally, one of the best sources for locating grant funding is the Internet. The Internet provides hundreds, if not thousands, of sites that contain excellent information regarding grants. Such information ranges from daily announcements, to useful statistics, to tips and techniques for writing grants, to current programs that are funded by grant dollars. Brewer, et al. (2001) identify 101 Hot Sites for Grantwriters (p. 108), several of which are listed below. The following 15 Internet sites and their corresponding URLs could very well provide you with the funding necessary to initiate a program or programs that could impact student success and achievement at your school. Review the listing, and then "bookmark" your favorite site(s) on your Internet work station. A tidbit of advice is offered to the "grant-seeker": The numerous sites that are identified and recommended often undergo changes and, as a result, the term "Under Construction" can very well indicate that a particular site may not be available. If so, move on to another site and source, and, as always, best of luck!

1. Grant Getter's Guide to the Internet—(http://web.calstatela .edu/ academic/orspgrantguide.html)

   This is a first stop for the novice grantwriter. This site provides an excellent compilation of useful information.

2. Guide to Funding: A Reference Directory to Public and Private Giving—(http://www.amherst.edu/~erreich/pcah_ stml/fundingguide.html)

   This is a beginner's website for learning about the numerous links to major grantmaking organizations, fundraising centers, and publications listings on grants and funding.

3. Scott Yanoff's Internet Connections—(http://www.sirius .we.lc.ehu.ed/internet/inet.services.html)

   This site is a super place for the novice Internet user to start seeking useful links to education sites that might provide potential funding resources.

4. Education Grants (Yahoo Web site)—(http://dir.yahoo.com/ education/index.html)

   A great website for the novice grant seeker.

5. National Science Foundation—(http://www.nsf.gov/ home/grants.htm)

   Excellent site for grantwriters interested in science and mathematics funding.

6. United States Department of Education Bulletin Board— (http://gcs.ed.gov)

   "Bookmark" this site for information related to current funding opportunities.

7. United States Department of Education: Guide to U.S. Department of Education Programs—(http://web9.ed.gov/GTEP/Program2.nsf)

   Visit this site that identifies every U.S. Department of Education program and potential funding links.

8. United States Department of Education Money Matters—(http://www.ed.gov/money.html)

   This site links grantwriters to discretionary grant application packages and other grants and contracts information.

9. United States Department of Education: What Should I Know About ED Grants?—(http://www.ed.gov/pubs/KnowAbt Grants/)

   "Bookmark" this site if you are a novice grantwriter seeking direct information to education grants.

10. (The) Foundation Center—(http://fdncenter.org/)

    This site links grantwriters to hundreds of private foundations and corporations that provide funding.

11. The Grants Library—(http://www.thegrantslibrary.com)

    This site houses the world's largest compilation of grant-oriented web resources.

12. Guide to Funding: A Reference Directory to Public and Private Giving for Artists and Scholars—(http://www.amherst.edu/~erreich/pcah_html/fundingguide.html)

    This is an excellent site worth visiting with web links to major grant-making organizations.

13. FEDSTATS—(http://www.fedstats.gov/)

    Statistics are provided by more than 70 federal agencies, and the site also includes a wealth of information for the grant seeker.

14. Fundsnet Services ONLINE—(http://www.fundsnetservices.com)

This extensive Web site provides 1,500 links to grants and fundraising resources.

15. Grants and Related Resources—(http://www.lib.msu.edu/harris23/grants/2educat.htm)

This Web site is great in providing the grantwriter with a significant listing of grants and funding sources for nonprofit organizations.

Fundraising

Additional school-site income is most frequently generated through the fundraising efforts of school-sponsored groups such as parent-teacher organizations and booster clubs, to name a couple. Parental involvement is essential for most school fundraising efforts. Parent groups and organizations provide a wide range of valuable services and activities, both inside and outside the school. However, the role of parents and parent-teacher organizations is often not specifically defined and as a result, problems—especially in the fundraising arena—often arise. What we do know, and appreciate as school leaders, is that the involvement of parents in schools can result in support for obtaining additional resources. The importance of parent organizations most often relates to their pressing desire to obtain quality services and resources for the schools they support. These "pressing" efforts are typically "reactive" rather than "proactive" and thus, proper training and guidance from school leaders is essential to ensure that parental efforts do not become administrative burdens or problems (Fullan, 2001).

Fundraising events typically involve the sale of different types of merchandise ranging from consumable items (candy, cookies, pizzas, or Thanksgiving turkeys, for example) to nonperishable items such as gift wrap, t-shirts, raffles, candles, senior rings, yearbooks, school picture sales, and just about anything else the fertile mind can imagine.

Fundraisers can generate significant income for a school, income that is above and beyond the standard district allocation. Fundraisers can also serve as monetary sources for purchasing items such as stage curtains, playground equipment, instructional supplies, and even air-conditioning for the school gym. However, if fund-raising efforts are not properly planned and organized, schools can very well be faced with numerous financial pitfalls (Mutter & Parker, 2004). For example, fundraising—while financially compelling and potentially rewarding—can quickly turn sour with lost, missing, or stolen merchandise and/or generated funds. This can publicly tarnish a school or embarrass an administrator in the eyes of the community, not to mention the district superintendent or school board.

To avoid such problems, the effective school leader must carefully follow either designated district policies and procedures or must proactively establish guidelines and regulations that allow for the proper management of fundraising merchandise, the selection of merchandise vendors, the designated responsibilities of those individuals involved, and the necessary bookkeeping systems that must be in place to protect a school's generated income and potential profit. By neglecting to do so, a school administrator is breaking one of the cardinal rules of school budgeting: Safeguarding school interests through the responsible stewardship of public funds, and setting and adhering to internal fiscal controls, both of which are best business practices necessary to protect school assets and personnel.

Expenditure Accountability and Control

One of the most important aspects of the school budgetary process is the accounting for and control of school expenditures. While expenditure accountability and control varies from state to state and from district to district, three closely related factors must be followed with strict and complete propriety: appropriate visionary planning, careful budgeting, and effective expenditure of school funds are crucial to ensuring that students benefit from a school's instructional program (Hack, et al., 2001). District and school-site expenditure accountability and control are aided by the use of a fiscal education and information management system, appropriate accounting procedures, activity income collection, deposit guidelines, timely payment of bills, and budget amendment practices. Each of these factors will be examined, and further consideration will be given as to how the interweaving combination of each factor contributes to effective and efficient school budgeting.

Fiscal Education and Information Management System

The fiscal education and information management system is an accounting and auditing process that is implemented in most states to control school and district budgets by utilizing a classification or codified structure (GASB, 2001). School districts as well as state departments of education need easy access to information directly related to the resources required to provide a fiscal infrastructure to support student learning. This codified information and management system electronically links revenues and expenditures, for example, from school to district office to state departments of education through an accounting process that traces and audits funding, examines programmatic considerations, and even reviews student achievement and accountability standards, as well as other important issues related to individual schools and districts. FEIMS can also detect material errors in the fiscal data of a school district and can further recognize and analyze the state-adopted fiscal accounting system that is required by state education code. Again, while certain aspects of a fiscal education and information management system may be utilized at local option, the overall structure is to be uniformly applied to all school districts in accordance with the Generally Accepted Accounting Principles (GAAP) as directed by the United States Department of Education and the Governmental Accounting Standards Board (GASB, 2001) in an effort to monitor and control expenditure accountability.

Accounting Procedures

The responsibility for wisely spending school funds to provide for a high-quality education for all students is further challenged by the precept that school dollars must also be actively and accurately accounted for and protected. The term *accounting* can be readily described as the process by which the effectiveness, legality, quality, and efficiency of budgeting procedures must be measured by the documented stewardship of all public funds (Thompson & Wood, 1998). While such a notion may have once been considered simply "good business" by schools and school districts, this same consideration, by today's budgetary standards, is a practical—if not essential—fiscal imperative.

Accounting procedures have been defined as the "fiscal imperative" method of determining whether a school has provided a fiscally valued and educationally valuable service to its clientele by emphasizing that school accounting procedures must serve to:

1. Monitor all incoming funds and outgoing expenditures in relation to the attainment of the school's vision, goals, and objectives.

2. Protect public dollars from any potential loss attributable to irresponsibility, wrongful utilization, theft, and/or embezzlement by any individual associated with the school or school district.

3. Provide for an assurance that public funds are being used to better ensure the academic achievement of all students.

4. Ensure that all legal requirements are followed implicitly.

5. Inform the general community of any and all facts and information regarding the fiscal solvency of the school-site and district.

In an effort to meet these accountability standards, the Governmental Accounting Standards Board (2001) issued a statement that emphasizes that accountability is the paramount objective of any budgetary process and, as such, all fiscal accountability reports must include information that (a) compares actual financial results with the legally adopted budget, (b) assesses the financial condition of a school or system, (c) complies with finance-related laws, rules, and regulations, and (d) assists in evaluating the efficiency and effectiveness of a school's or district's fiscal budget and educational program.

Finally, the National Center for Education Statistics (2005) identifies several standard accounting practices that serve to guide schools and districts in their common goal of accounting for public funds in relation to the budgetary process.

1. Define and utilize account classifications and codes that provide meaningful financial management information.

2. Comply with the Generally Accepted Accounting Principles as established by the Governmental Accounting Standards Board.

3. Recognize and utilize accounting technology, and safety and security procedures.

4. Comply with all state and federal laws and fiscal accountability reporting requirements.

By adopting and following these standards, school leaders allow for the continuous monitoring of expenditures as well as accountability and control of budgeting procedures—all of which are most definitely considered to be "best practices" for further ensuring that students are benefiting from school appropriations. Equally important, all school personnel are protected from any potential legal entanglements that are often associated with the mishandling of district dollars.

Collection and Deposit Structures

The school leader, who also serves as the budget manager, quickly realizes that the basis for effective budgeting is not only the planning aspect of the budgetary process but the proper accounting of income collected and deposited as well. Good budgeting must be based on a structure of collections and deposits that helps to further establish an accounting control mechanism to preclude any monetary mistakes and possible theft or embezzlement. Such a structure is imperative since most schools have activity accounts that are based on the collection of funds from school clubs, booster organizations, general fees, and numerous other dollar-generating initiatives.

The School Activity Account

The school activity account is one important area of the budgetary process where sound financial practice must be exercised. Many administrators will confide that there are two problematic areas that can get a school leader in serious trouble—sex is one, and money is the other—especially when an activity account is involved. The school activity account can very well be the one budgetary consideration that poses the most serious financial complications and implications. For example, the activity account at many schools (high schools in particular) can generate significant income from revenue sources such as fundraisers, vending machines, school pictures, athletic receipts, library and textbook fines, numerous student fees, school store operations, field trip receipts, appropriated district funds, and the list can go on and on.

Since thousands of dollars flow through a school's activity account in most states, administrators have the primary fiscal responsibility of not only managing such a budget but also complying with federal and state laws and district policies and procedures (Brimley & Garfield, 2005). School activity funds must be safeguarded, and prudent verification of all accounts within the activity fund must be monitored and audited for the purpose of ensuring that such monies are appropriately utilized for the benefit of the students served.

School administrators must also understand that the school activity account can quickly become a nightmare if appropriate bookkeeping practices are not in place, followed, and maintained. Funds that are collected from various school-related activities must be accounted for as money received and spent in relation to the different activity accounts in which said dollars have been allocated. For example, money that has been collected from ticket sales related to the school athletic banquet should be placed in the athletic account; money that is collected from the sale of school pictures for the purpose of postal services should be placed in the postal account. Now, let's return to the issue of bookkeeping practices and the development of an income collection and deposit structure.

Components of the Collection and Deposit Structure

The purpose of any collection and deposit structure is to establish budgetary controls to prevent general accounting mistakes, blatant theft, and/or embezzlement of funds. This structure is composed of several components which identifies key personnel who should be bonded prior to collecting, accounting for, and depositing funds. The term *bonded* relates to a legal process known as *surety bonding*, which is frequently defined as a guarantee of performance. In other words, a bonding agency will reimburse a school district for any financial loss related to fraud, theft, or embezzlement that might occur as a result of an individual who has been entrusted with the handling of funds (Brimley & Garfield, 2005). Returning to the components of collection and deposit, a carefully crafted budgetary structure should include and ensure:

1. Cash Receipts Collections—When generated dollars, typically in small denominations, are brought into the school office by an activity sponsor, at least two bonded individuals should collect, count, and account for the funds. In this manner, the total amount of cash and checks submitted should accurately match the receipts presented and also match the amount listed on the receipt given to the sponsor.

2. Activity Account Postings—Following the cash receipts collection, the monetary amount should be counted and double counted, again by bonded personnel and then entered into the bookkeeping system. If the system is computerized, a summary cash receipts report is automatically generated and provides the bookkeeping staff and school leader with a listing of the receipt entries, as designated by date, along with the dollar amount of said receipts and the specified activity account (athletics, school pictures, library fund, for example) into which the collected receipts are to be entered.

3. Bank Deposit Procedures—Following any account posting, it is highly recommended that a bank deposit slip be prepared

immediately. Then, a third bonded individual (someone different than the two individuals who are collecting, accounting, and preparing the deposit slip) should be selected to place the funds in a deposit bag and promptly directed to make the necessary bank deposit. Many school districts require that two individuals take any deposits to the bank. While such a procedure is not absolutely necessary, it is a wise practice. The bank depository procedures help ensure that the amount of money received totals the daily deposit and further reduces the possibility of human error, theft, and/or embezzlement.

4. Bank Reconciliation Processes—The bank reconciliation process reveals much about the management of a school's budgetary practices. Proper reconciliation of bank statements and records is considered one of the most important fiscal safeguards available to a school leader. Bank reconciliation is nothing more than a check-and-balance system that ensures that the school's bank statement matches the data recorded in the school's financial records. This process, while considered by many to be tedious and time-consuming, provides an opportunity for the school leader to identify differences that may exist between bank records and school records. This process goes beyond the trust factor to a method of verification by providing for a monthly analysis of the school's financial records. School leaders should be cognizant of the possibility that problems associated with the school's bank statement could very well signal financial problems elsewhere—in other school accounts for example, or with the school's accounting procedures. Mutter and Parker (2004) have noted that "repeated, irreconcilable differences between a bank statement and the school's books may indicate incompetence or fraud" (p. 17). Nothing could come closer to the truth, and every school leader should recognize that such possibilities can and do exist in schools, and, as a result, the administrator, as the budgetary manager, should be ever vigilant.

Understanding each of the specified components as well as the need for income collection and deposit is an essential element of the budgetary process and one which must be mastered by the school administrator in order to prevent fiscal problems that could lead to the ending of what may very well have been a successful and most satisfying administrative career.

Timely Payment of Bills

One of the most often overlooked aspects of expenditure control is the timely payment of bills. Timely payment of bills can actually be a source of revenue as such a practice often translates into the collection of a discount. In other words, vendors often offer discounts for early payment. For example, many vendors provide for a 15% discount if the bill is paid within 30 days or a 10% discount if the bill is paid within 60 days. For any school administrator to avoid or ignore the possibility of early payment of bills is to neglect the potential of controlling expenditures and, more important, keeping school money in school pockets. When a vendor discount is earned, that is money saved, and money saved is simply ensuring that there are funds for further allocation to meet other important educational needs.

Some administrators might suggest that the payment of bills accrued by each school is the responsibility of the district's business office and that there is little that can be done beyond the school site. We beg to disagree! The effective school administrator should work to ensure that his or her bookkeeping clerk regularly contacts the business office department in charge of payment of bills. This method of reminder can very well encourage business department personnel to "speed-up" the payment process, and, as a result, a discount is collected, an additional expenditure is controlled, and the money saved remains at the school level.

Budget Amendments

Flexibility has often been the operative term associated with school budgeting. Those administrators who carefully manage and monitor the school budget come to an early realization that all purposeful planning combined with the best of intentions can quickly go by the wayside when academic goals and objectives change for the betterment of the students served. For example, consider the following scenario: During the course of the school year, additional funds are allocated to the school due to a significant increase in unexpected student enrollment. An "above-basic" allotment is transferred to the school by district administration at the conclusion of the first semester to make up for the financial strain that the increased enrollment is imposing on the educational program, let's say, in the area of technology. The computer lab is equipped to serve 25 students when in reality, due to the increased student enrollment, the smallest class using the lab has no fewer than 33 students. Any school administrator will be clamoring, if not demanding, supplementary technology funds to meet the need to purchase additional computers and computer stations. Therefore, an adjustment or amendment to the school budget is needed to facilitate the incoming new dollars and to account for the funds—especially when an upcoming expenditure is about to occur.

When such amendments are necessary, the school administrator must move funds from one account to another in a method of correcting a previous posting by transferring a portion, if not all, of a balance from one account to another. Again, consider the technology scenario and note that the "above-basic" allotment, provided to the school to adjust for the unexpected increase in student enrollment, is transferred from the district level to the school and placed in the Supplies and Materials account. At the school level, the funds are needed for desktop computers and required furnishings. Therefore, an adjustment or amendment must be made with the funds being transferred to the proper accounts—Computer Labs and Furniture and Equipment. To facilitate the transfer of any funds and to further amend the school budget, many administrators utilize either standardized forms or memorandums that have been approved by the school district (see Forms 5.1 and 5.2). These forms, often completed online, serve as a method of budgetary accountability and most certainly provide the necessary documentation to ensure that the adjustment and/or transfer will occur.

Budget amendments are an essential part of the budgetary process and are utilized in an effort to move funds from one account to another and at times to correct an accounting error that has been made. We strongly recommend that the school leader follow any district budget amendment instructions and procedures by making wise decisions with regard to income and expenditure adjustments and transfers, and by completing the appropriate paperwork involved in the budget amendment process. While budget amendments are often necessary, the effective school administrator readily learns that the overuse of the adjustment and transfer process can send questionable signals to, and raise serious inquiries from, business department personnel, district-level administrators, and even school board members, who in many systems have final approval over budgetary changes.

Form 5.1   Sample Budget Amendment Request (Standardized Form)

STAR Independent School District
Budget Amendment Form

School or Department: Star Middle School

From Account # 199-11-6399.00-041-06	Amount $10,000.00	Previous Budget $38,055.00	Current Budget $28,055.00
To Account # 199-11-6637.00-041-06	Amount $10,000.00	Previous Budget $2200.00	Current Budget $12,200.00
From Account # 199-11-6399.00-041-06	Amount $5000.00	Amount $28,055.00	Current Budget $23,055.00
To Account # 199-11-6639.00-041-06	Amount $5000.00	Amount $1000.00	Current Budget $6000.00

Campus Action Plan Goal/Objective/Activity or Need Addressed:

Goal IV: Provide an intensive, technology-centered language development curriculum that emphasizes the learning and application of oral/written communication skills at all grade levels.

Objective 1.6: Explore and implement accelerated instructional program with resources that will increase overall student achievement.

Activity 2.3: Upgrade the technological equipment and facilities.

Justification for Budget Amendment:

Star Middle School plans to amend a portion of its allocated funds from the Supplies and Materials account and transfer said funds to the Computer Lab account to purchase desktop computers, and to the Furniture and Equipment account to purchase computer stations to better meet the campus need for additional technology equipment as related to the recent increase in student enrollment. Consequences of nonapproval would hinder our ability to increase student achievement in the area of language arts and language development because the current computer hardware and furnishings are inadequate, again due to the significant increase in student enrollment. Implementation would begin immediately during the second semester of the 2008-2009 school year.

Originator	Date Requested
Principal	Date Approved
Director of Budgeting	Date Approved

Form 5.2   Sample Budget Amendment Request (Letterhead
                 Correspondence)

STAR Middle School

"Committed to Excellence"

TO: Director of Budgeting, STAR ISD

FROM: Dr. Ed U. Kator, Principal

DATE: January 12, 2009

SUBJECT: Budget Amendment Request

The following transfer of funds is being requested:

Amount	From Account Number	To Account Number
$10,000	199-11-6399.00-041-06	199-11-6637.00-041-06
$5,000	199-11-6399.00-041-06	199-11-6639.00-041-06

Campus Action Plan Goal/Objective/Activity or Need Addressed:

Goal IV: Provide an intensive, technology-centered language development curriculum that emphasizes the learning and application of oral and written communication skills at all grade levels.

Objective 1.6: Explore and implement accelerated instructional program with resources that will increase overall student achievement.

Activity 2.3: Upgrade the technological equipment and facilities.

Budget Amendment Justification:

Star Middle School plans to amend a portion of its allocated funds from the Supplies and Materials account and transfer said funds to the Computer Lab account to purchase desktop computers, and to the Furniture and Equipment account to purchase computer stations to better meet the campus need for additional technology equipment as related to the recent increase in student enrollment. Consequences of nonapproval would hinder our ability to increase student achievement in the area of language arts and language development as the current computer hardware and furnishings are inadequate, again due to the significant increase in student enrollment. Implementation would begin immediately during the second semester of the 2008–2009 school year.

Approved by: _____

Budgeting Director, STAR Independent School District

Budgetary Systems

Chapter 1 outlined the differences between school finance and school budgeting. School finance is often associated with stringent fiscal policies and accountability procedures. School finance, simply put, is the process by which funding to support public schools is raised and distributed (Guthrie, Garms & Pierce, 1988) On the other hand, budgeting has been defined by Brimley and Garfield (2005) as a process that involves planning, allocation, and expenditure of funds, and a continuous monitoring and evaluation of each of the pieces within the process. This working definition correlates quite effectively with *The Budget Plan* section previously examined in this chapter.

The school budget serves numerous functions, often depending on which system of budget administration a school district uses. The most common budgetary systems, which are typically prescribed by state education code or local board policy, include function/object budgeting, zero-based budgeting, and school-based budgeting. Each system has particular strengths and weaknesses, but all are intended to serve several important functions including a projection of proposed sources, allocations, and expenditures of funds for the next fiscal year. While budgetary administration and budget systems go hand-in-hand, it must be noted that each varies from state to state and all must be appropriately administered and evaluated within the confines of standard accounting practices as defined by the United States Office of Education in the *Financial Accounting for Local and State Systems Handbook* (2003) and correlated with the Generally Accepted Accounting Principles as established by the Governmental Accounting Standards Board.

Function/Object Budgeting

This particular administrative system of budgeting is based on a process whereby anticipated expenditures are entered into the budget ledgers through a codified and electronic process. Funds within this administrative system are budgeted according to *function* (instruction or administration or health services, for example) and *object* (supplies and materials or payroll or professional and contracted services, for example). This system is used by many school districts across the nation since it is the required format of most state and federal education agencies (see Table 5.3). The function/object budgetary system also closely aligns with the fiscal education and information management system of each state.

Table 5.3   Function/Object Budgeting and Coding

199 – **11** – **6339**.00 – 041 – 08 – 30

The _function code_ is an accounting entity that identifies the purpose of any school or district transaction.	The _object code_ identifies the nature and object of an account or transactions. For example: payroll, supplies and materials, capital outlay.
Function **11** refers to _instruction_. Thus, this particular code represents a transaction that will impact the instructional program of a school or district.	Object **6339** refers to _technology supplies and equipment under $5000.00_. This particular object code is found under the main object heading (6300) entitled: _Supplies and Materials_.

The strength of function/object budgeting correlates with the administrative need of schools and districts to exercise the maximum amount of fiscal control over funds especially when numerous individuals are responsible and accountable for the budgeted dollars. The function/object budgetary system also readily provides for quick and easy administration of the school budget and further allows for sensible decision making in relation to the general analysis of cost and benefit factors associated with evaluating specific instructional programs and programmatic expenditures in relation to student academic gains and achievement.

A weakness frequently attributed to the function/object budgeting system is the system's strongest point. Function/object budgeting, while providing for analysis and evaluation of programs and expenditures, unfortunately lacks specificity as well as depth and detail necessary to aid with the often essential and ongoing analysis that is so critical in mandated evaluations of differing instructional programs.

Zero-Based Budgeting

Following the 1977 U.S. Supreme Court ruling, _Serrano v. Priest_, a budgetary system known as zero-based budgeting gained popularity in states such as California, New Mexico, Texas, and others where educational inequities existed in state funding formulas, processes, and procedures (Dayton, 2002; LaMorte, 2005). This system of budgeting is based on the most advantageous concept of involving all parties in the budgetary decision-making process with school administrators and teams carefully analyzing budgeted line items, whether each is currently in place or is being newly proposed. Beginning the budget development process with zero dollars, the learning community, with administrative guidance, is charged with ranking all budgetary considerations in priority order, then choosing potential alternatives based upon funding allocations, and further annually evaluating all programs that are associated with the accompanying budget.

The downside to zero-based budgeting is the significant amount of time, effort, and paperwork associated with the process as well as the fact that there are only so many dollars appropriated by the school district. Many school districts and administrators—often to the dismay of the learning community—decide that this particular budgetary system is too cumbersome and complicated, especially when compared to other budgetary preparation systems.

School-Based Budgeting

School- or site-based budgeting is a system similar in concept to the zero-based budgetary system. It, too, incorporates the idea of involving all parties in the budgeting effort for the betterment of student achievement and school reform. This system of budgeting gained credible recognition during the late 1980s and early 1990s by providing the learning community—especially faculty and staff—with serious and legitimate input into the school budgeting process. School-based budgeting has been described as a decentralized system of providing appropriations for all aspects of the school program (Wohlstetter & Buffett, 1992). For example, school staff can often impact the final decision as to what areas of the school budget will be funded and for what amount. Such areas can include the instructional program, instructional supplies, equipment, textbooks, library books, travel, professional development and, in some instances, the distribution of school personnel salaries.

One potential benefit of the school- or site-based budgeting system is the ongoing analysis of student needs in relation to teaching resources and budgeted dollars. The effectiveness and efficiency of this system relates to the essential planning and recognition, by all parties, of those educational factors (socioeconomic status or ethnicity, for example) that can impact or influence student achievement. Such a budgetary system is advantageous because it enables the school-site team to exert significant influence not only on the budget development process but also on school policy and programmatic decisions as well. In addition, this particular system of budgeting is considered to positively impact the morale and climate of a school since many individuals within the learning community are actively involved in the decision-making process. Finally, school- or site-based budgeting can very well serve to increase the academic achievement of students (Malen, Ogawa & Kranz, 1990).

Another important consideration associated with the school- or site-based budgeting system relates to an understanding that district administrators must rethink the "top-down" approach to school budgeting and decision making and assume a more facilitative role at the school level in the budget preparation and decision-making processes. Typically, district administration continues to determine, monitor, and evaluate allocated dollars associated with maintenance, cafeteria, and transportation services. Responsibility for these areas of educational management often requires additional and more specified expertise that extends beyond that of the instructional leader and site-based team.

The downside to the school- or site-based budgetary system relates to three considerations: (1) the addition of parents and community members in the budgetary decision-making process requires significant training and learning for all the constituents involved; (2) equity among differing schools may be endangered as some school's budgetary decision-making process reflects greater participation and advocacy of the constituents; and (3) certain budgetary decision-making procedures as related to personnel, for example, can bring potential legal entanglements.

The advantage of any or all of the budgeting systems identified within this chapter relates most importantly to the implementation and utilization of the site-based decision-making model and process and to an understanding that while each budgetary system can be effective, no single system is necessarily better than the other. Herman and Herman (2001) pointedly assert that "no school system should settle for one budgetary approach when a combination of all budget systems can be utilized for a thorough evaluation, on a cost/benefit basis, of the programs and activities offered the students at each school building" (p. 20).

Accounting and Auditing Procedures

Proper accounting and auditing procedures have been described by Thompson and Woods (2001) as "a protection for districts, boards, administrators, and everyone affected by the business of education"

(p. 130). Such an assessment is absolutely correct since the two terms, accounting and auditing, go hand-in-hand and serve as the critical elements in best protecting individuals and organizations from financial wrongdoing, suspicion, accusation, and even innuendo. Auditing serves four functions: (1) Auditing makes good business sense—audit investigations are essential to determining if appropriate and legal expenditure of funds has occurred. (2) Auditing and the accompanying regular investigations provide written documentation to school administrators, superintendents, and board members who must be kept abreast of the financial dealings of the district and schools. Such documentation provides proof to the educational constituency (parents, taxpayers, state and federal governmental agencies) that the fiscal integrity of a school or district is sound, intact, and following the dictates of law. (3) Auditing helps to detect human and technical error in the accounting process. In any school system, large or small, errors will occur, and the audit investigations delineate between accidental and intentional errors. (4) Auditing can be the guiding force that brings about necessary change to accounting procedures and financial operations in need of improvement.

While several types of auditing procedures have been developed to provide a system of checks and balances to an educational organization, the two most common are internal and external auditing.

Internal auditing is a self-checking process that typically provides for monthly reports to the school board. These reports detail the financial status of the school district and in most instances reveal expenditures of the differing schools within a district. Internal auditing is generally a continuous examination of a school's and district's accounting system in which a multiple approval process is incorporated to safeguard against error or fraudulent practices.

External auditing is the formal accounting process by which a school's financial records are examined by a qualified and independent accountant—typically a Certified Public Accountant. External audits are generally ordered on an annual basis with an accounting firm spending anywhere from two to six weeks conducting an extensive and exhaustive investigation that checks revenues and expenditures and further compares cash balances against encumbrances and thus ensures that all statutory and legal requirements are in good order. External audits provide audit reports and findings in written and presentation formats as well as fiscal and accounting recommendations to superintendents and school boards. Audits serve as a measurement of the trust factor in any educational organization by validating the fiscal management (good or bad) of a school system. The auditing process is more than good business, it is money well spent to better ensure the sound fiscal stewardship of a school and school system.

Fraudulent Practices

Fraudulent practice in the education business may not be an everyday occurrence, however, newspaper stories regularly reveal that many a dishonest and unethical employee often manages to divert thousands of dollars from a school's activity account into the pockets of the unscrupulous embezzler. When school personnel hear district gossip about such capers but realize that these types of dealings are not making the local newspaper or evening newscast, this is usually associated with the fact that school systems do not want to provide unsolicited attention and unsettling fodder for community consumption. However, if you are a school leader of any tenure, you quickly recognize that embezzling can very well happen during your watch. Therefore, the possible advent of such fraudulent actions makes it worth your while to learn a little more about the subject and should further cause the educational leader to examine the school's recordkeeping and auditing procedures to best negate any tempting prospects and looming loopholes.

Fraudulent practices are closely akin to an individual's ethical decision-making process as revealed in Chapter 2 and Chapter 7. Beckner (2004), for example, examines the topic of responsibility and two relatable considerations: discretion and accountability. He notes that a school leader should exhibit discretion and accountability by exemplifying a level of responsibility that appropriately and discretely follows school policies and procedures.

Accountability standards, which exemplify the highest levels of ethical conduct, must also be maintained. A perfect example was unfortunately showcased in a school district where an associate superintendent for business and financial affairs entertained colleagues at a local men's club and subsequently charged lap-dancing expenses, to the tune of $2,000 in a single visit, to the school district's credit card. The expectation for responsible behavior and personal ethical standards quickly went by the wayside. The cost for such a personal indiscretion: the loss of the associate superintendent's professional reputation and the subsequent public humiliation of the individual and his family. The district also suffered both internal turmoil and external criticism. This, in turn, negatively affected the public's confidence in the school district's leadership team and several school board members. Ultimately, the community outcry resulted in numerous administrative resignations, and several school board members who ran for reelection went down in defeat (Osborne, Barbee, & Suydam, 1999).

Embezzlement

Embezzlement has been defined as the fraudulent appropriation of property by an individual to whom it has been entrusted (OMB, 2005). The operative term within this definition is "entrusted." The embezzler is usually a trusted employee who is taking advantage of a school leader's confidence or a school leader's lack of attention to detail. Embezzlers have a method of operation, a thinking process, that is frequently thrust upon unsuspecting schools and school systems. Embezzlers often believe that they are smarter than the school leader, and they generally perceive themselves as being someone who can outwit a less-than-sterling school business department.

Common schemes are typically quite simple to employ because the trusted employee has generally won the confidence of a school leader. In fact, the best embezzlers are often the individuals who are given more authority than a position dictates. These same individuals have also realized that the ability to embezzle is only limited by their own imagination. Most embezzlement at the school level involves the pocketing of actual cash that is received.

The receipt of cash at a school office is quite common—especially in relation to fundraising programs and efforts. The theft of cash is quick and easy, and it is most difficult to detect. This act is accomplished by the embezzling employee who simply doesn't enter the cash receipt in the accounts receivable records. A perfect example involves cash received from a school activity or from a club sponsor who is less interested in the details associated with record keeping and thus simply trusts the administrative office clerical staff to "count this for me please, I've got to get back to class—my students are taking a test!" To prevent this scenario and the associated monetary temptation, a school principal should insist, if not demand, that all cash received be accompanied by a written receipt of the calculated dollar amount, and a cash receipt must be provided by the "trusted" employee to the club or activity sponsor immediately upon receipt of the cash funds.

Another preventive step is the "spot-check" process instituted by the school leader. This process further assures that the cash received is the cash recorded. In other words, the school leader needs to purposefully check on a regular basis with differing school activity or club sponsors to determine when funds are coming into the school and most notably into the school office. The school leader should also carefully monitor the bookkeeping records, always looking for suspicious signs of fraud and theft. The school leader should also understand that unexpected internal audits by district business office personnel can often prevent employee embezzlement efforts.

Finally, never underestimate the vulnerability of a school or district to an act of embezzlement. An ounce of prevention may very well be the cure for the common scheme. Effective school leaders must recognize the following 10 precautionary practices that can very well inhibit and discourage acts of embezzlement.

1. Ensure that the individuals who expend monies are not the custodians of accounting for said monies.

2. Review all bank statement reconciliation procedures.

3. Keep two separate and independently maintained sets of bookkeeping records as related to receipts and expenditures.

4. Provide for effective and appropriate reconciliation of receipts and accounts.

5. Never sign blank checks before leaving for a conference or vacation.

6. Develop and utilize bookkeeping policies or regulations.

7. Utilize bonded employees only.

8. Cross-train office personnel to perform bookkeeping responsibilities.

9. Utilize an independent accountant to conduct regular internal and external audits.

10. Review on a regular basis with office staff the detailed expectations for appropriate and ethical office bookkeeping standards and procedures.

Other Risk Factors

While an incident of monetary theft or embezzlement may not be directly tied to you, the school administrator, a public perception will definitely exist that such a fraudulent practice occurred on your watch and therefore you share in its responsibility. Some school leaders have taken a lax approach to the budgeting process by delegating all or parts of the budget and accompanying tasks to others or by simply deciding that "instruction is my bag" and as a result, have either neglected or ignored the budgetary process all together. Such thinking or action can very well be considered a costly risk factor, if not an ultimate criminal mistake.

Hughes (2002) examined a Center for Creative Leadership report which studied the topic of career derailment, in other words, how leaders fall short of the personal success predicted earlier in their careers. Three different but quite compelling causes of career derailment quickly came to light when examined in relation to fraudulent practices at school: (1) failure to constructively face an obvious problem, issue, or circumstance; (2) mismanagement; and (3) inability to select trustworthy subordinates. With these three causes for career derailment, we would like to pose to the school leader three interesting questions for consideration as related to the risk factor of monetary theft or embezzlement: (1) Do you perceive the fraudulent problem being the result of the leader's actions or inactions? (2) Do you perceive the leader was aware of the consequences of their actions or inactions? (3) Which of the three causes do you perceive would most likely lead to the career derailment of an educational leader from the perspective of a fraudulent practice at school?

Appropriate auditing and accounting procedures, while not completely foolproof in eliminating the potential for fraud and embezzlement, do serve to assure the educational clientele of the fiscal state of a school and district, and such procedures further discourage unethical practices. Effective school leaders understand that any misuse or misappropriation of school funds can quickly destroy the public trust. Most important, the effective school leader acknowledges that any and all unethical and fraudulent activities can very well derail, if not promptly conclude, a career that was once perceived to be most promising and long lasting.

Final Thoughts

The budget development process, with its numerous components, is a legal mandate in most states. Effective and efficient budgeting practices are dependent upon skillful school leaders who know more than budgetary management. School leaders must not only understand fiscal accountability and control, collection and deposit structures, budgetary systems, and accounting and auditing procedures, these same school leaders must realize how the visionary component of school-based planning integrates with the budget development process and how all work collaboratively to build a stronger academic program which in turn positively impacts student achievement.

The budget development process is more than implementing and utilizing effective and efficient fiscal practices. The budget development process is an integral part of the visionary and planning process by which the members of the learning community all have a voice, a stake, a right to impact the academic success of all students. So many years ago, long before the concept of school-based budgeting gained popular acceptance in our schools, Roe (1961) revealed that the school budget is the translating of "educational needs into a financial plan which is interpreted to the public in such a way that when formally adopted it expresses the kind of educational program the community is willing to support, financially and morally, for a one-year period" (p. 81). Such sentiment couldn't be expressed any better some decades later, except to say: Unlike Mr. Getty, we hope educational leaders find allocating money to support academic goals to be a considerable pleasure!

Discussion Questions

1. What is the purpose of a budget plan and how does it interact in relation to the school action or improvement plan within the budgetary process?

2. Identify at least two sources of income that a school leader and team can generate; discuss the pros and cons of each; and further explain how these sources relate to the visioning and planning aspects of the school budgeting process.

3. Which of the components of the collection and deposit structure are essential to the budgetary handling of the school activity account? Support your answer.

4. Consider the purposes of accounting procedures and explain how such practices can assist schools in their quest of accounting for the expenditure of public funds.

5. Which budgetary system has your school or school district adopted? Discuss how this particular system further commits your school or district to the site-based decision-making and management approach.

6. What precautions should a school leader take with regard to the possibility of embezzlement? In what ways is your school vulnerable to this budgetary risk factor and how would you as a school leader address the identified vulnerabilities?

7. Fraudulent practices have been described as being "closely akin to an individual's ethical decision-making process." How does ELCC/ISLLC Standard 3, identified in Chapter 2, support this statement?

8. You have recently been named as a new school leader. Outline your responsibilities as related to effective and efficient budgetary practices, and further explain how the learning community (faculty, students, parents, external patrons, etc.) should be involved in the development of the school budget.

Case Study Application: Sex, Money, and a Tangled Web Woven

Dr. Edgar Buchannen was principal at Fullerton Peak High School in the suburban community of Gibsonville and had been in this position of instructional leadership for nearly five years. He had previously experienced a very successful principalship at Woodson Middle School in a major metropolitan area just north of the state capital. Dr. Buchannen had worked diligently with his new faculty to raise student academic achievement from low performing to a significantly higher state department standard of accountability. Such a task had not been easy, but Dr. Buchannen was convinced that he and his team—along with the students at Fullerton Peak High—had jumped a most difficult hurdle.

In the interim, Dr. Buchannen had developed a great working relationship with Lisa Nicoles the school's bookkeeping and attendance clerk. The two had "clicked" from their first day together, and they really appreciated each other's work ethic. One Saturday morning, Eddie—as he had asked Lisa to call him—came in early to catch up on some budgeting issues while Lisa was completing the student demographic information needed for the next scheduled round of statewide testing. Both were pleased to see one another working on the important tasks at hand, and soon they took a break to enjoy a morning doughnut and cup of coffee. Lisa complained of a neck ache from working all morning to enter the demographic data into the computer system, and Eddie, quickly offered to massage her neck. Lisa did not demur.

Well, you've heard the story before—all too common in our business—and we need not go any further other than to reveal that such an act quickly led to serious complications. Over the next few months, a steamy affair developed although the two tried to keep any suggestion of impropriety away from the office.

Unfortunately, Lisa's marriage was falling apart, and although Eddie was married with three children of his own, the two carried on their secret romance. With Lisa's failing marriage, she had developed—along with her husband who had a serious gambling problem—credit card debts to the tune of $125,000. She was in deep trouble since these financial complications were in her name, and the collectors were demanding payment or repossession of tangible assets. What she needed was cash, and she needed it fast. While the romance grew so did a little problem that Lisa had at work—she was regularly taking money from the school's different activity accounts such as athletics, drama, band, choir, and even the "cola wagon" which took in hundreds of dollars at the varsity football game each Friday night.

Dr. Edgar Buchannen had no idea of these embezzlement efforts until one evening when Lisa broke down in tears and told him that he needed to help her get out of this financial predicament. He grew furious and stated: "Help you! Wait a minute, aren't you the one stealing from the district? Don't involve me in your petty theft crimes!" Lisa, with a steely-eyed stare, retorted: "Don't play games with me, 'Mr. Self-Righteous.' You're the one cheating on your wife, you two-faced fraud. You help me or else!"

Thus began a criminal partnership conceived in a mutual distrust of one another, and based on some very questionable ethical and moral standards. From that point forward, a dangerous game of "borrowing" money, with every intention of paying back the stolen funds, escalated to a point of no return. The "borrowed" dollars never found their way back into the accounts, and the "cover up" only lasted until someone in the district business office caught on to a scheme built on lies, deceit, misjudgment, and unethical practices.

Application Questions

1. What probable repercussions will Dr. Edgar Buchannen and Lisa Nicoles face as a result of their actions? Explain the "risk factors" associated with their behaviors.

2. Cooper (1998) examines two approaches to maintaining responsible conduct in organizations: internal and external controls. External control has been described as responding to an unethical situation by developing new rules or rearranging the organizational structure or establishing more cautious monitoring procedures. Internal control is often described as increasing preservice and inservice training programs, or placing ethical leadership discussions on local meeting agendas. Which of these two policy perspectives would best be associated with this case study and why?

3. What legal implications are at issue in this case study? Which laws, education codes, or board policies have been broken or infringed upon? Give specific examples and explanations.

4. From the perspective of a school leader, how could the act of embezzlement presented in this case study have been prevented? Identify specific precautionary practices you would incorporate.

5. Northouse (2004) defines ethics as a "system of rules or principles that guide us in making decisions about what is 'right or wrong' and 'good or bad' in a particular situation." He further stipulates that ethics provide "a basis for understanding what it means to be a morally decent human being" (p. 302). Is Dr. Buchannen a morally decent human being? Support your answer.

6. What is the possible impact of such actions, as described in the case study, in relation to the school district? Support your response from both a budgetary and political perspective.

6

Building the School Budget

All of us are smarter than any one of us!

—W. Edwards Deming

Site-Based Decision Making

Norton (2005) states: "Today, leaders of organizations are expected to be knowledgeable of the political world in which organizations operate and to be highly skilled in working with the dynamics of political competition, conflict, decision making and control" (p. 227). Such a statement exemplifies the parameters by which school leaders utilize differing strategies for working with the learning community.

One of the most effective strategies to be incorporated by a school leader is the SBDM process, as this approach to school leadership is superior to the autocratic process (followers do not play a role in defining the problem or in generating a solution or decision), exceeds the consultative process (followers are consulted but the leader makes the decision), yet is reflective of the group process (followers in collaboration with the leader reach a consensus relative to a solution to the dilemma or decision presented). What we do know about decision making relates to the concept that a high-quality decision has a direct and measurable impact on an organization (Hoy & Miskel, 2005). In the case of public schools, when the SBDM process is properly implemented, there is a total quality component to a decision—generally one in which the decision made has improved services to the clientele—the students, parents, faculty and staff, and the overall learning community. Visioning, planning, developing, implementing, and continuously evaluating a school budget must be an extension of the leader-follower collaborative decision-making dimension. Recall the words of Edward L. Bernays: "Disraeli cynically expressed the dilemma when he said: 'I must follow the people. Am I not their leader?' He might have added: 'I must lead the people. Am I not their servant?'" (*Columbia*, 1996).

During the 1980s, public schools began to shift to a business purpose approach, incorporating business principles into program planning, daily operations, and an overall reform movement in response to concerns about the quality of education in America (Webb, 2006). This paradigm shift, as applied to school fiscal matters, was associated with the decentralization of district budgets. During the late 1980s and early 1990s, W. Edwards Deming's "total quality" principles were infused into the mainstream of public school reform efforts. The term "quality," like integrity, fairness, and ethics—as discussed in Chapter 2—was then, and often continues to be difficult to define, although everyone claims to know quality when they see it. John M. Loh states that the definition of quality is quite simple: "It is a leadership philosophy which creates throughout the entire enterprise a working environment which inspires trust, teamwork, and the quest for continuous, measurable improvement" (*Columbia*, 1996). While Loh's definition serves as a start for understanding the school budgeting process, a more practical and working definition of "quality" might be identified as a continuous process that is achieved through a change in organizational culture. In other words, a school leader must ensure that the budgeting process, in collaboration with site-based decision making, is never-ending (continuous) by transforming the shared norms, values, or beliefs (culture) of a school into one in which the leader becomes a facilitator, and the followers become active participants. Therefore, the school leader, for the betterment of the organization, must place emphasis on total quality through the empowerment of others by utilizing participative decision making, by articulating a vision, and by involving many in the planning and development stages of a school budget. Hence, "all of us are smarter than any one of us." This change process is one that makes the work of schools more intrinsically motivating and thus, more appealing, rather than one of a controlling nature in which the members of the learning community are extrinsically motivated as a result of a "top-down" attitude and approach (Hughes, et al., 2002).

Why Site-Based Decision Making?

The site-based decision-making process is crucial to building an effective and efficient school budget. First, all actions regarding the budgetary process are considered, assessed, evaluated, and approved in a public forum with all interested parties involved. Site-based decision making is most appropriate in this time of intense scrutiny and accountability. Most school leaders would welcome the opportunity to showcase the sensitive subject of public fund expenditures and the overall school budget in an open forum. Second, when utilizing site-based decision making, the budgetary process is "above board." In other words, there are no hidden funds or secret accounts. Third, all represented and interested parties are involved, and thus private and personal agendas meet with little merit and have a tendency to go by the wayside. Fourth, current research reveals that decentralizing four key resources (power, information, knowledge, and rewards) can enhance organizational effectiveness and productivity (Hadderman, 2002). Hadderman further stipulates that "highly involved schools need real power over the budget to decide how and where to allocate resources; they need fiscal and performance data for making informed decisions about the budget; their staff needs professional development and training to participate in the budget process; and the school must have control over compensation to reward performance" (p. 27). Finally, and perhaps most important, budgetary decisions must be made on a "student-first" basis. For these reasons alone, it only makes sense to incorporate the site-based decision-making model into the budget development process.

Who Builds the School Budget?

The authors of this text strongly support the idea of all parties being actively involved in the development of a school budget. This is a collaborative process that involves the school leader doing more than just calling a group of representatives together for the purpose of reviewing the already completed school budget. Appropriate training, supervision, guidance, and direction—in a most confident, energetic, intelligent, creative, tolerant, adjustable, dependable, and social manner—must be the leadership norm in a systematic budget development process. Note the words of Alex Cornell: "The real world is a messy place—yet, even a messy place should be attacked systematically" (*Columbia*, 1996). The building of a school budget must involve all parties who, working collaboratively, develop the budget from a more specific, systematic, and decision-making perspective.

Recall from Chapter 4 and Chapter 5 that the academic action or improvement plan is useless unless it is directly integrated with the budget plan. Working collaboratively with the school leader, representatives of the learning community begin determining the educational needs of an organization in relation to the allocated funds. Sound budgeting theory dictates the involvement of all parties representative of the learning community. Unfortunately, the active participation of members of the learning community in the budgetary process has been given significant lip service by numerous school leaders when, in fact, such collaboration is often minimal in practice. Considering this assessment, let's examine which stakeholders should be involved in the budget development process and further identify their respective roles and responsibilities.

The School Leader

The school leader at the site-level is often considered the most important individual in the budgeting process. School leaders today can be described as having considerable more years of teaching experience prior to assuming their first administrative position (Doud & Keller, 1998), and are increasingly female at both the elementary and secondary levels—making up to 20% of high school principals, compared with 12% in 1988 and 7% in 1978 (NASSP, 2001). Administrators of color continue to be underrepresented in our public schools with only 2.6% Black and less than 1% Hispanic (Banks, 2000).

Today school leaders view their role as being hurried, overburdened, and frustrating with more responsibility, less authority, and increasingly stressful (Sergiovanni, et al., 2004). Specifically, the school leader has been described as being "sandwiched between what state and district policymakers intend, what the superintendent directs, what parents expect, what teachers need, and what students want" (Cuban, 1988, p. 76).

What is needed in terms of school leadership reform is a distributed leadership model as described by Ogawa and Bossert (1995). This model closely correlates with the SBDM process in which leadership does not reside in specific roles or with specific persons, but in the relationships that develop between the differing individuals in social, cultural, and instructional roles and responsibilities. In other words, leadership at the school level must be participative and shared. Keeping these descriptors in mind, one can recognize that the school leader plays a very important role in the budgeting process. Now, let's delve deeper into a school leader's role and responsibility in developing the school budget.

School-Site Administrators

Differing administrators, with differing titles and responsibilities—principal, assistant principal, site specialist, campus facilitator—often make budgetary decisions. These individuals may very well serve as the school's budget manager. As previously noted within this chapter, budgetary decision making can occur as follows:

1. By autocratic method and manner. (My way or the highway!)

2. By involving a select group of individuals. (Those who understand best!)

3. By working in collaboration with a site-based decision-making team. (Again, "all of us are smarter than any one of us!")

We believe that the latter is the best approach to building a school budget because those who have worked collaboratively in developing an academic action or improvement plan should be responsible, along with the school leader, for determining the budgetary needs of the organization. In this process, the school leader or designated leader provides the SBDM group with the necessary forms and figures indicating previous and current year budget allotments and expenditures. Budget histories can be very useful in providing fiscal information to all parties involved. This information is essential in understanding how budgeted allotments and expenditures have influenced and impacted student achievement over a period of time.

Next, the school leader should seek teacher and staff input by asking for the submission of inventory requests for specific supplies, materials, and other educational needs that are essential to the establishment of an exceptional instructional program. Faculty and staff who have been accustomed to an autocratic approach to the school budgeting process may not be initially thrilled about this new approach to building the school budget because it may seem to be a waste of valuable time since their ideas and suggestions have never been sought or implemented before. However, with the passage of time and with proper guidance, the team will begin to realize that the process is worthwhile, that their input is actually being sought, valued, and utilized to determine what expenditures are important in providing the best possible learning environment, and that the school leader is genuinely interested in their ideas and input.

Interestingly, as time goes by, the school leader realizes that the faculty and staff are in many respects the best persons to evaluate optimal considerations for the teaching and learning process. Again, with proper training, guidance, and leadership, "buy-in" in relation to the budgeting team comes quite easily. The days when the budgeting process was described as too complex, or a time when a "chosen few" were the only ones able to develop a budget, or the "tight-ship" era when authoritarian rule was the norm are soon forgotten and a new era of collaborative decision making and participative leadership become boldly institutionalized within an organization's culture.

Finally, once the necessary input has been collected, a budget meeting is scheduled, and the process of bringing recommendations for budgetary expenditures begins in earnest. Building a school budget, from a school leader's perspective, is a step-by-step process that ultimately culminates in a document that has been developed in collaboration with representatives of the learning community. This document, when properly prepared, contains more than just the budgeted dollars. It is a document that allocates funds for the best instructional methods and programs which further ensure the academic success of all students.

Other Committee Members

Let's examine the one question often posed by school leaders in relation to the budgetary process: Which individuals should serve as the site-based team members on the budget development team? The answer varies from school to school. Some states and school districts define the parameters of the site-based decision-making process and the budget development team. For the sake of further discussion, let's define the site-based decision-making/budget development team membership as being those individuals (elected and/or appointed and voting and/or nonvoting members) who are representative of the learning community. Such contributing members could very well be teachers who represent each grade level or departments, as well as band, choir, orchestra, drama, and athletic directors, paraprofessionals, custodians, parent-teacher organization representatives, parents, military liaisons, community members (chief of police, for example), school administrators, central office administrators (directors of curriculum, special education, bilingual education, gifted and talented education, maintenance and transportation, and business operations, for example) as well as comptrollers or business managers, and even the superintendent of schools. The key to identifying committee members is inclusive representation of the learning community. Now, let's examine the differing members and their roles more closely.

School-Site Directors

Band, choir, orchestra, and drama directors should be automatically represented on the budget development team since these individuals often serve as budget managers with responsibilities related to instruction, extracurricular issues, purchasing musical instruments and materials, uniforms, costumes, and the cost of transportation. The building-level athletic director can very well serve on the team to help coordinate expenditures related to the athletic program and to further supervise costs associated with transportation, coaches salaries and stipends, officials, uniforms, ticket-takers, police, ambulance, doctors, and meal and lodging expenses (Herman & Herman, 2001).

Teachers and Grade-Level or Department Chairs

These teachers and other certified personnel should be an integral part of the school committee because these individuals know and understand the students and the instructional programs, and they are the professionals who most affect a school's culture and climate which serves to impact the students' ability to excel and achieve. Grade-level or department chairs are generally the most informed and best prepared to lead the instructional program, and thus, their areas of expertise qualify them to effectively make budgetary decisions.

Central Office Administrators

These administrators may be required at times to serve on the school committee when their particular area of expertise and advice is needed. Central Office administrators are generally nonvoting members who can prove to be very helpful when certain topics outside the committee's level of expertise are being discussed and examined.

Students

Often overlooked, students (typically grades 6 and above) can provide legitimate advice and consideration as related to the budgetary process. Who knows better what is most relevant, timely, and workable in relation to student issues and, in some instances, programmatic considerations?

Community Members

Those members from outside the school often provide the insight that only an "outsider" can visualize. Many times school administrators and faculty are myopic when it comes to school and programmatic issues. Sometimes, whether we like it or not, the "outsiders"—the community members—can present a long-overlooked or often ignored perspective that, when addressed, can have a positive and long-lasting impact on school reform, improvement, and most important, student achievement.

School Budget Applications

Ovsiew and Castetter (1960), in their classic account, *Budgeting for Better Schools,* suggest that there are several integrating aspects of a school budget that can serve to ensure better budgets for better schools. Their book—while nearly half a century old—may be dated; however, their message is not. Examine the noted budgetary components and applications that are essential to building an effective school-based budget. By following this prescribed and step-by-step process, the school leader can experience a sense of security that his or her proposed budget should meet with appropriate recognition and approval at the district-level budget hearing and defense session.

Descriptive Narrative—A detailed description of the school (years of operation, location, demographic information such as percentage of free and reduced lunch population, federal program eligibilities and identifiers, and other important descriptors such as socioeconomic backgrounds and poverty status of the student population) serves to identify in narrative form the areas of budgetary need and consideration.

Programmatic Identifiers—Identifiers relating the grades of the school, number of total students enrolled, ethnic distribution of students, and other programmatic considerations (special education, gifted and talented, bilingual education, vocational education, etc.) along with the number of faculty employed—by teachers, counselors, nurses, administrators, librarians, paraprofessionals, clerks, secretaries, etc.— are detailed in this particular budgetary narrative.

Mission Statement—A statement of introduction as related to the school's goal or philosophy about the nature of learners, learning, and the purpose of the school serves to explain the rationale of the organization and how that rationale impacts the decision-making and budgetary process.

Student Enrollment Projections—A chart or table utilizing the Cohort Survival Method (see *Projecting Student Enrollment* in this chapter) is used to project student populations that are critical to any school budget as future student enrollment increases or decreases. Increases or decreases in student enrollment are most indicative of the funding necessities essential for a school's success.

Analysis of Academic Action or Improvement Plan—When analyzing the academic action or improvement plan of any school, consider the following questions:

1. What aspects of the instructional program need improvement?

2. What pertinent sources of data verify any areas of improvement?

3. Which of the concerns, problems, or needs are the most significant for improving the overall instructional program?

4. Which of the proposed improvement efforts are within the school's budgetary scope and capability for effective action and implementation?

5. Which of the concerns, problems, or needs are of the highest priority and is there a sound research base for addressing each prioritized concern, problem, or need?

Needs Assessment/Priority Analysis—A needs assessment and priority analysis serve to identify what areas or aspects of the school program need improvement after a review of all pertinent sources of data (e.g., academic action plan, previous studies, local and statewide test results, survey of teachers, students, and parents). In addition, a review of the research literature along with collaborative team discussions regarding each area of instructional and/or programmatic concerns, are particularly useful and beneficial.

Teacher/Student Distribution Table—This table (see Table 6.1) indicates the distribution of students by grade level in relation to the number of staff dedicated to serving said students from a programmatic consideration (e.g., bilingual classrooms, inclusion-monolingual classrooms, and monolingual-only classrooms). This table provides for a visual understanding of why and how an increase or decrease of students enrolled can impact the budgetary allotment for teacher salaries, paraprofessional assistance, and program development.

Table 6.1   Teacher/Student Distribution Table

	Bilingual	Inclusion-Monolingual		Monolingual Only		
Pre-K	15 t & ta		15 t & ta			
Grade K	22 t	5 + 10 t & ta	21 t	22 t	22 t	22 t
Grade 1	21 t	5 + 10 t & ta	22 t	22 t	20 t	21 t
Grade 2	20 t	5 + 10 t & ta	21 t	22 t	22 t	
Grade 3	22 t	5 + 10 t & ta	22 t	22 t	20 t	21 t
Grade 4	20 t	4 + 10 t & ta	22 t	21 t	22 t	
Grade 5	28 t	5 + 15 t & ta	31 t	35 t	33 t	32 t
Spec Ed			43 2 t & 5 ta			
# Students	148	29 + 65	197	144	139	96
# Staff	7 t 1 ta	6 t 6 ta	9 t 6 ta	6 t	6 t	4 t

t = teacher   ta = teacher aide or assistant

Faculty Distribution Table—This table (see Table 6.2) reveals a distribution of the entire faculty in relation to the number of assigned personnel to a school. This table allows the school team as well as central office and business department administrators to visualize areas of need in relation to the student enrollment projections.

Above Basic Personnel Request and Justification—The Above Basic Personnel Request narrative is a necessary component of the budgetary process as this particular section of the school budget justifies the need for increased faculty and staff. Furthermore, this narrative seeks those critical funds for additional personnel which may be above the basic school allotment.

Allocation Statement—The allocation statement serves to provide in tabular form (see Table 6.3) a brief, but descriptive, distribution of funds. Within this statement the total student population count is noted along with the Average Daily Attendance (ADA) or Average Daily Membership (ADM) rate. In addition, the statement identifies the ADA or ADM funding on a per-pupil basis along with the special education, gifted and talented, bilingual/ESL, Title I, and state compensatory funding allocations. Finally, a total allocation is listed. This total allocation is the basis for building the school budget.

Table 6.2   Faculty Distribution Table

Position	No. Assigned to Campus
Principal	1
Assistant principal	1
School secretary	1
FEIMS clerk	1
Instructional facilitator	1
Counselor	1
Nurse	1
Nurse assistant	1
Librarian	1
TOTAL faculty	9

Position	No. Assigned to Campus
G/T teacher	½
Speech therapist	½
PE teacher	1
Music teacher	1
Office aides	2
Title VI aides	1
Custodians	4
Food services	5
TOTAL faculty	15

Table 6.3   Allocation Statement: Mountain Vista Elementary
School—Distribution of Funds

		State Allocation			Campus Allotment
Student population	=	818			
Average Daily Attendance	=	90%	818 × 0.90	=	736.2 = 736
ADA Funding	=	736	× $2,537.00	=	$1,867,323.00
Special Education	=	72	× $7,125.00	=	$513,000.00
Gifted and Talented	=	45	× $285.00	=	$12,825.00
Bilingual/ESL	=	148	× $237.50	=	$35,150.00
Title I (82%)	=	671	× $262.50	=	$176,137.00
State Compensatory	=	671	× $475.00	=	$318,725.00
Total Allocation				=	**$2,803,837.00**

Distribution of Funds Table and Narrative—This section of the school budget is dedicated to detailing in tabular form (see Table 6.4) with the exact distribution of funds. This section is presented in a line-item format with general narrative descriptions (e.g., human, material, fiscal resources) revealing how the funds will be expended.

Final Budget Compilation—The final budget compilation is to be completed in a tabular format as dictated by the school district and on the forms provided by the district business department. If the school district does not specify the format or provide the necessary budget compilation forms, the use of the Microsoft® *Excel* software program is a recommended method, although other marketed versions are readily available. The final budget compilation should utilize the fund, function, object, subobject, organization, fiscal year, and

Table 6.4   Distribution of Funds: Mountain Vista Elementary School

Salaries

Teachers, nurse, librarian	=	$37,500
Principal	=	$62,000
Assistant principal	=	$54,000
Counselor	=	$45,000
Diagnostician	=	$46,000
Instructional facilitator	=	$47,000
Speech therapist	=	$42,000
Testing coordinator	=	$40,000
Security officer	=	$32,000
Secretary	=	$23,000
Instructional/clerical aides	=	$20,000
Nurse assistant	=	$20,000
Custodian (head)	=	$30,000
Custodian	=	$23,000
Food services	=	$7,500
Consultant(s)	=	$1,000 per day

Supplements (Stipends) = $1,500

Resource (Special Education)	Head nurse
Bilingual	Head counselor
Math	Head custodian
Science	Department chairs
Librarian	Diagnostician
Home Economics	

program intent codes (see Chapter 1, as well as Resource B: *The Budgeting Codes Activity,* for examples).

Budget Allocations

Budgetary allocations are derived from a variety of revenue sources as previously examined in Chapter 1. These sources—federal, state, and local—provide the funding dollars associated with budgetary allocations and are generally identified as governmental fund types with descriptors such as General, Special Revenue, Capital Projects, and Debt Services (Williams, 2004). The two most important governmental fund types insofar as the school budget allocation is concerned are General and Special Revenue. General funds are typically available for school allocations with minimal planned expenditure and purchasing restrictions. General funds are needed to sustain the normal operations, administration, and counseling expenditures of a school. Special Revenue funds are governmental funds used to account for the proceeds of specific revenue sources that are legally restricted to expenditures for specified purposes. Examples include Title I (Improving Basic Programs), Vocational Education, and Food Services. Dollars from these funding sources are then utilized as the basis for budgetary allocations at the school level.

School budget allocations are typically based on an average daily attendance or an average daily membership formulation. ADA versus ADM is a school finance issue regarding the relationship between student attendance and financial support. Determining the allocation by ADA benefits school districts with higher attendance and penalizes those with lower levels of attendance. The more students in attendance equates to more money for districts. In addition, more students in attendance equates to more learning taking place, a fact supported by test scores. Proponents of ADM as the basis for funding, cite the fact that whether or not the student is in attendance on any particular day, the costs of district operations (salaries, utilities, transportation, other services, etc.) remain constant, and that the allocation of funds should recognize such (Funkhouser, 1999). Nevertheless, the allotment (based on either of the formulations)—along with additional dollars that may be appropriated as a result of the number of identified Limited English Proficient (LEP), Gifted and Talented, Special Education, and At-Risk students—serves as the initial basis for school allocated funds. Additional allotted monies for the school can come from grant dollars, technology funds, maintenance funds, staff-development allocations, and other miscellaneous allotments. While most of these allotted dollars to the school budget allow for administrators to implement and control activities authorized by the budget, certain limitations—if not restrictions—can be placed on the budget for the following reasons:

- The budget limits the type, quantity, and quality of instruction provided at the school level.
- The public is critically interested in education and more specifically, instruction.
- School operations are often diverse and broad in scope and thus important budgetary planning is necessary for effective and efficient expenditure of funds.
- School allocations provide direction for the school's future.

Now, let's examine those allotted funds that are restricted in the scope of their expenditure usage.

Restricted Funds

While budget allotments can be used for a variety of services and expenditures at the school level, some are more restrictive than others. In addition, once basic school allotments have been appropriated to particular operational areas within the budget, all funds come under certain function restrictions and can only be used for that designated purpose unless district approval has been sought, typically in the form of a budget amendment.

Restricted funds are often associated with Title I, bilingual education, and special education dollars and programs. For example, many school districts carefully restrict the expenditure of funds appropriated to these particular programs on the basis of federal and state guidelines which often stipulate that funded dollars within these particular budgeted categories can only be utilized for the purpose of student-related instruction. Consider the following scenario.

The office secretary needs a new file cabinet, desk, and carpet but recognizes that the general funds allocated have already been appropriated and encumbered within the budget. However, the school administrator notes that the Title I accounts have just enough monies to be appropriated for the needed office upgrades. Thus, in an electronic instant, the Title I funds are encumbered and plans are made for a quick purchase of the needed office items. No doubt, creative thinking on the part of the school administrator has occurred, and such action brings to mind the old adage: "Necessity is the mother of invention." However, the Title I funds must be utilized for Title I eligible students, and chances are the justification for incorporating Title I funds for the purchase of new office equipment for the school secretary would be a real stretch of the imagination in relation to the dollars utilized.

Therefore, the concept of restricted funds brings us full circle in terms of understanding the need for accounting code structures which have been determined and designated by the Governmental Accounting Standards Board. These accounting code structures ensure that a sequence of coding is uniformly applied to all schools and school districts to account for the proper appropriation and expenditure of public funds (GASB, 2001).

Coding Applications

States require that a standard fiscal accounting code system be established in accordance with state law. Such a coding structure is to be implemented and uniformly utilized by all local school districts in accordance with generally accepted accounting principles. States require that a standard fiscal accounting code system be adopted by each school district. The system must meet at least the minimum requirements prescribed by state boards of education and must also be subject to review and comment by state auditors. In addition, the accounting system utilized by states and school districts must conform to the Generally Accepted Accounting Principles (GAAP). This system has been identified by the Governmental Accounting Standards Board (2001). A major purpose of the fiscal accounting code system is to ensure that the sequence of codes is uniformly applied to all school districts across a state. The budgetary accounting code system is a labeling method designed to assist with the accuracy and legality of expenditures. School budgets are tracked by state education agencies via the budgetary accounting code system.

School district accounting systems are organized and operated on a fund basis. A fund is an accounting entity with a self-balancing set of accounts recording financial resources and liabilities. A school district designates the fund's financial resources for a distinct purpose. The fund's purpose may be established by the state or federal government as well as the local school district. Previously identified in Chapter 1 and shown again in Table 6.5 is an example of a state's operating accounting code structure as well as explanations which serve to describe the specifics of each code in particular. Further noted in Table 6.6 through Table 6.10 are examples of certain categories for fund codes, function codes, object codes, organization codes, and program intent codes.

Table 6.5   Example of a State's Operating Accounting Code Structure

199	11	6399.00	001	08	11

1	2	3	4	5	6	7

Fund codes **(1)** have three digits with the first digit identifying regular, special, and vocational programs, for example. A second fund digit denotes either the grade level or particular program area or category such as the local operating fund. The third digit can further define the type of program in relation to student classifications, type of services rendered, and/or student population. For example, the number 211 identifies the Title I federal fund group.

Table 6.6   Categories for Fund Codes

Fund Codes—1st Digit (Nine Categories)

100 –   Regular programs

200 –   Special programs

300 –   Vocational programs

400 –   Other instructional programs

500 –   Nonpublic school programs

600 –   Adult and Continuing Education Programs

700 –   Debt service

800 –   Community service programs

900 –   Enterprise programs

000 –   Undistributed expenditures

Function codes **(2)** are typically two to four digit numbers which further designate budget program areas (see Table 6.7). Function codes represent as many as nine different categories. For example, the most commonly used function code category within a school budget is instruction, although other areas including school leadership, guidance counseling, and health services are frequently incorporated as well.

Table 6.7   Categories for Function Codes

Fund Codes—Nine Categories

10 –   Instruction and instructional-related services

20 –   Instructional and school leadership

30 –   Support services – student (pupil)

40 –   Administrative support services

50 –   Support services – nonstudent based

60 –   Ancillary services

70 –   Debt service

80 –   Capital outlay

90 –   Intergovernmental charges

Object codes **(3)** are three to four digit numbers used to further describe program allocations and expenditures. Object codes represent seven different categories (see Table 6.8). The object codes represent within the budget the nature or object of an account, a transaction, or a source.

Table 6.8   Categories for Object Codes

Object Codes—Seven Categories

6000 –   Expenditure/expense control accounts

6100 –   Payroll costs

6200 –   Professional and contract services

6300 –   Supplies and materials

6400 –   Other operating costs

6500 –   Debt service

6600 –   Capital outlay – Land, buildings and equipment

Subobject codes **(4)** are used as accounting entries to delineate, for example, secondary-level departments like English, Mathematics, Science, Physical Education, History, and so forth.

Organization codes **(5)** are three-digit numbers that identify accounting entries within a budget as being high school, middle school, elementary school, superintendent's office, or school board (see Table 6.9). This code readily notes which high schools in a district are the oldest or the newest. For example, Elm High School (001) is the first or oldest high school, followed by Birch High School (002), Oak High School (003), and Hickory High School (004), so forth. The same coding designation is true for middle and elementary schools as well.

Table 6.9   Categories for Organization Codes

Organization Codes—Two Categories

001-699–	Organization units – Schools
700–	Organization units – Administrative

Fiscal year codes **(6)** identifies the fiscal year of any budgetary transaction. For the 2007-2008 fiscal year of a school district, the digit 08 denotes the fiscal year.

The program intent code **(7)** is frequently represented by two digits and is used to designate the rationale of a program provided to students. This code is used to account for the cost of instruction and other services that are directed toward a particular need of a specific set of students. There are 11 program intent codes, as identified in Table 6.10.

Table 6.10   Categories for Program Intent Codes

Program Intent Codes—Eleven Categories

11 –	Basic educational services
21 –	Gifted and talented
22 –	Career and technology
23 –	Special education
24 –	Accelerated instruction (at-risk programs)
25 –	Bilingual education
26/27–	Nondisciplinary alternative education programs
28/29–	Disciplinary alternative education programs
30 –	Title I

Special Activity 1: Utilizing Accounting Codes

Using Tables 6.6 through 6.10, consider what accounting code would be utilized to complete a school requisition form as related to the following situation. Write your answer in the blanks provided.

_____–____–_____–_____–____

The Special Services department has requested additional mathematics manipulatives to be utilized in several classrooms at Maple High School. These needed supplies could very well help increase the overall mathematic test scores at the second oldest high school in the

Mapletown Independent School District, as the statewide account-ability system now holds all schools accountable for the academic achievement of special education students. (Answer provided at the conclusion of this chapter.)

Special Activity 2: Utilizing Accounting Codes

Carefully read and assess the scenario presented and then apply the proper accounting codes by referring to *Accounting Codes Reference Sheet* found in Resource B.

Kit Monami, assistant principal at Eagletown High School was designated as the budget manager by her principal this school year. Kit was quite competent in her new role and found working with the budget team and the school budget to be quite challenging, yet most interesting. In her role as budget manager, she had to interact with the differing high school departments and the many demanding per-sonalities. Most recently, Clay Harrison, the head football coach at Eagletown High, had asked Kit if his request for additional athletic supply funds had been included in the budget for the upcoming school year. He was particularly concerned about the need for additional supplies for the equipment room. In fact, he needed several video cas-sette tapes to use in filming the defensive line during after-school practice. "How else does the district expect us to win if I can't video the weekly progress of the team?" the coach inquired. Kit explained that she needed Coach Harrison to calculate the cost of the video tapes, complete the necessary requisition form, and then she would determine if there were additional funds still available in the speci-fied account within the school budget.

In this scenario, as Coach Harrison completes the budget requisi-tion form, consider the proper coding for each category: fund, func-tion, object, subobject, and program intent code and then fills in the Fund Account Number found on the requisition form as noted in Form 6.1. (Answer is provided at the conclusion of the chapter.)

Projecting Student Enrollment

Student enrollment information is of major importance to schools and school districts specifically in relation to declining or increasing enrollments. The effects of declining enrollments can be most detri-mental to a school budget. Consider the following in relation to a decline in a school or district enrollment: reduced state aid; hiring freezes or reductions in force (RIF); smaller class sizes thus creating

Form 6.1   Sample Requisition Form

Eagletown Independent School District
"Home of the Soaring Eagles"
100 Eagle Nest Drive
Eagletown, USA

REQUISITION FORM

Requisition No. _____

Purchase Order No. _____

School _____   Originator _____

Fund Account Number _____ – _____ – _____ . _____ – _____

STOCK #	QTY.	QTY. SHIPPED	DESCRIPTION	UNIT COST	TOTAL COST

Merchandise Received by _____ $ _____
Total Amount

Approved by _____   Date _____

the need for fewer teachers; redistricting of school boundaries, and the possible closing of school facilities. Increasing enrollments can create overcrowded classrooms, and a need for rapid staff and facilities expansion (Castetter, 1996).

Therefore, accurate enrollment projections are vital to budgetary allotments, staff planning, and facilities utilization. Over the years, numerous methods have been incorporated by school districts to project student enrollment. The most common model to date remains the *ratio retention* or *cohort survival method*. Furthermore, an important report on enrollment projection procedures revealed that the cohort survival method provides results that continue to be sufficiently accurate (Phi Delta Kappa, 1989). Today, the cohort survival method is frequently utilized in schools in the form of computer software programs developed by companies such as Ecotran Systems, Inc., of Beachwood, Ohio, Educational Data Systems of San Jose, California, and Education Logistics, Inc., of Missoula, Montana (Webb & Norton, 2004).

School leaders should recognize that most central office administrators prefer to underestimate enrollment projections because the potential cost to a school district is less (Seyfarth, 2005). This is important to know since under projections can equate to less than an appropriate and necessary allocation to the school, as well as the potential for understaffing the school.

Table 6.11 describes the cohort survival method. It is important to note that procedures required to project student enrollments are of three types: gathering demographic data, analyzing the data for possible trends, and then projecting student enrollment on the basis of the evaluated findings. In addition, a careful review and examination of all external environment information is critical to making accurate enrollment projections. Listed below are several considerations as related to external environment information:

- Emerging communities to include rental properties such as apartment complexes and mobile home parks
- Changing population patterns
- Nonpublic school enrollments
- Open school enrollment policies
- Initiation of voucher plans
- A significant public event such as the loss of a major community employer
- Mobility rate

The cohort survival method accounts for the number of students enrolled in each grade level in a school or across a district over a

Table 6.11 Projecting Student Enrollment (Cohort Survival Method)

Directions: Review the list of procedures for utilizing the cohort survival method to better understand the process of projecting student enrollment. Following these procedures, and noted in Table 6.12, is a partially completed worksheet that can be utilized for practice purposes.

1. Begin the cohort survival method by incorporating previous school year data. For the purpose of initiating this particular activity, as noted in Table 6.12, the 2004–2005 school year has been fictitiously inserted. In figuring the formula, set your calculator to round up (>0.5) or down.

2. Recognize that the kindergarten enrollment for the 2004–2005 school year is 88. The first-grade student enrollment for 2005–2006 is 115.

3. Now, using your calculator, divide the 2005–2006 first grade student enrollment (115) by the 2004–2005 kindergarten student enrollment (88). This calculation will reveal a ratio of 1.31.

4. Use the worksheet noted in Table 6.12 to calculate the ratio for the remaining set of numbers.

5. Following the calculation of ratios, add each ratio in each column in Table 6.12 and divide by 4 to determine the average ratio. The average ratio for the first column is 1.12.

6. Again, using your calculator, multiply the 2008–2009 kindergarten enrollment (90) x the average ratio (1.12) which equates to a first-grade student enrollment projection of (101) for the 2009–2010 school year.

7. Continue your calculations for each grade-level for the 2009–2010 school year.

8. Now, continue to calculate student enrollment projections for the 2010–2011 school year by multiplying the kindergarten enrollment x the average ratio. Remember to not calculate ratios for years starting with 2008–2009.

9. Further project student enrollments by adding across the *Projecting Student Enrollment Worksheet* (Table 6.12) to obtain the total student enrollment for each school year.

10. While there is no one method of projecting student enrollment to provide an absolute calculation, the cohort survival method has proven to be one of the most accurate formulas since the early 1950s.

NOTE: The information utilized in Table 6.11 was adapted in part from *Human Resources Management for Effective Schools* (2005) by John T. Seyfarth and from the author's personal experiences utilizing the Cohort Survival Method at the school district level.

Table 6.12   Projecting Student Enrollment Worksheet

Enrollments by Grade Levels

School Year	K	1	2	3	4	5	TOTAL
2004–2005	88	110	99	91	96	101	585
ratio	1.31	1.00					
2005–2006	93	115	110	96	99	109	622
ratio	1.06	.90					
2006–2007	91	99	103	112	109	115	629
ratio	.99	.97					
2007–2008	85	90	96	89	95	107	562
ratio	1.11	.97					
2008–2009	90	94	87	91	98	104	564
Average Ratio	1.12	.96					
2009–2010	82 x 1.12	101 x .96	90				
2010–2011	84 x 1.12	92	97				
2011–2012	77 x 1.12	94					
2012–2013	72 x 1.12	86					
2013–2014	75	81					

specified number of years. Moreover, it requires a school to account for the number of students expected to enroll in kindergarten over the next five years. This accounting of potential kindergarten students is based on census data or housing surveys of children between the ages of 0 and 4 who reside in the school or district attendance zone. This information drives an average ratio calculation for each class from year to year. This average then allows for future-year enrollment projections (Castallo, et al., 1992).

Finally, Castetter (1996) suggests that it is important that all enrollment projections follow the guidelines identified below:

- Two separate projection models or methods should be utilized: one at the district level and one at the school level.
- Incorporate at the district level the cohort survival method to better account for student enrollment trends and community variables.
- Develop enrollment projections at the school level as well.
- Always monitor at the school level any enrollment changes. Monitoring means doing a student survey, for example, just prior to the close of the school year. Monitoring also suggests conducting housing surveys—especially if new construction projects, such as apartment complexes, are being built. One-bedroom apartments, for example, are typically designed for single dwellers with no children, while two- and three-bedroom units represent family dwellings and are thus indicative of a potential increase in student enrollment.

Important Budget Considerations

Barbara Hutton once stated what is obvious in life and in the practice of effective and efficient budgeting: "So, you want to take it with you—well, I've never seen a Brink's truck follow a hearse to the cemetery" (*Columbia*, 1996)! While an individual can save as much money as possible, at some point in time those saved dollars must be spent, given away, or inherited by someone because, as Hutton said, "You can't take it with you!" The same holds true in school budgeting—spend it or give it back. We suggest that you spend your allocated dollars but do so in the most accurate, effective, and efficient manner possible. With this thought in mind, consider the following "top-ten" priority list when it comes to working with the school budget. At the conclusion of each list, identification (in parenthesis) of district or school site responsibility is denoted.

1. Utilize a budget calendar—The purpose of the budget calendar is to ensure that the budget development process is continuous. The school leader who follows the guidelines and dates associated with a budget calendar maximizes the possibility that nothing interferes with budgetary preparation requirements or the best interest of the school and school system. (District)

2. Identify budgetary allocations and restricted funds—Know and understand the revenue sources and how such impact the

school-budgetary allotment. Recognize that allotments can be based on an average daily attendance formulation and know how critical it is for the school leader to continuously monitor the enrollment of all students as well as those students served in special programs, i.e., Bilingual Education, Title I, Special Education, and Gifted and Talented. Realize that certain funds have specified restrictions associated with appropriateness of expenditures and student services. (District and school site)

3. Project incoming and exiting student populations—The effective school leader regularly monitors incoming and exiting student populations as the student enrollment of a school can significantly impact the budget allocation. In addition, accomplished school leaders learn to utilize the Cohort Survival Method as a process of projecting student population five years into the future. (District and school site)

4. Project faculty and staff increases and reductions—Any increase or reduction in faculty and staff strongly correlates to student enrollment. By utilizing the Cohort Survival Method to forecast into the future, the school leader can readily assess how many faculty and staff will be needed to ensure a strong educational program. (District and school site)

5. Conduct a needs assessment—Efficient needs assessments allow a school leader to recognize which interventions were most effective in increasing student achievement and cost the least. (School site)

6. Receive input from all parties—Effective school leadership incorporates collaborative strategies which in turn generates the involvement and input from organizational followers. When collaborative decision making is implemented, visioning, planning, evaluating, and the overall budgeting process generate measurable improvements, all of which ultimately serve to benefit students, faculty, and the organization. (School site)

7. Project and prioritize expenditures—Consider all line-item accounts within the budget including supplies and materials, salaries, and capital outlay, for example, when analyzing and prioritizing budgetary expenditures. The school leader who actively monitors and regularly evaluates the budget is able to project and prioritize expenditures within the budget that center on specified objectives which are correlated to the

instructional program, the school action plan, and the overall vision of the learning community. (School site)

8. Build the budget—Exceptional budgetary leaders regularly meet with the budget development team in an effort to create a school vision, develop a plan of action, and then build the budget itself. This level of quality leadership serves to demonstrate the following outcomes so necessary in the budget development process:

   - Knowledge of the complete budget process
   - Knowledge of the amount of funding available and where the budgetary allotment is derived
   - Knowledge of collaborative decision-making procedures and processes as well as the proper protocol involving the input of all parties
   - Knowledge of accounting codes (School site)

9. Defend the school budget—Skilled leadership and knowledge of the school budget permits an administrator to exercise ingenuity and competence in addressing questions, suggestions, and criticisms of the school budget at a budget defense hearing. Effectively defending the budget is an act of elucidating clear points and explicating proper justifications for the budgetary decisions made. Such actions in the formal budget defense hearing reveal leadership traits of credibility and expertise. (District and school site)

10. Amend and adjust the school budget—Even with all the purposeful budgetary planning and careful monitoring and evaluation, no administrator can expect the school budget to remain on target without certain adjustments being made during the course of a fiscal year. Budget amendments are necessary when unexpected circumstances and situations inevitably arise. Having a working knowledge of the amendment process will facilitate the need to move funds from one account to another without leaving an impression of budgetary incompetence or mismanagement. (District and school site)

The Budget Calendar

School administrators recognize that effective budget development is based on the concept of continuous evaluation. This recognition also brings about the need for the development of a specific and detailed budget calendar. The budget calendar lists critical dates for the preparation, submission, review, and approval of the school budget. A variety of straightforward techniques are generally used in developing a budget calendar. While the details involved in developing a school budget are not the same in all districts, it is recommended that the following steps be considered and incorporated when preparing a new budget calendar:

1. Develop a master calendar to ensure that all budgetary actions and activities are consistent and compatible across the district and from school to school.

2. Identify specified budgetary actions and activities for inclusion in the calendar and then arrange them in chronological order.

3. Assign completion dates for each action and activity and note them on the budget calendar. These completion dates should be assigned by working backwards through the actions and activities from legally mandated dates as stipulated by state law and local district policy.

4. Assign dates and space them accordingly to ensure that sufficient time is allowed for the completion of each action and activity listed on the budget calendar.

5. Identify on the budget calendar specifically who is responsible for each action or activity listed. This procedure is particularly useful to school administrators because it identifies their own specific responsibilities and task completion dates.

Again, the budget development process and proposed calendar will vary from state to state and district to district as fiscal year beginning dates will start anywhere from July 1 to September 1. School officials who fail to establish a budget calendar or who procrastinate the budget-development process are making a serious mistake, because the avoidance of approaching deadlines will definitely interfere with conscientious budget-building efforts (Brimley & Garfield, 2005).

Outlined below is a proposed budget calendar with specified considerations as related to the budget development process:

Schedule	Procedure
Prior to February 1	The superintendent of schools establishes the budget planning format and schedule for preparation of the next fiscal year budget.
	Person Responsible: Superintendent
February 1	A Budget Request by Function and Object form should be distributed to school administrators for completion by March 1. Columns for "Actual Previous Year" and "Estimated Current Year" should be completed prior to the form being disseminated to the administrators responsible.
	Person Responsible: Associate Superintendent for Finance
February 15	Projected student enrollments should be developed.
	Person Responsible: Associate Superintendent for Administration in collaboration with school leaders
March 1	School administrators should return the completed Budget Request by Function and Object form to the district administrator responsible for the initial review and consideration of school needs.
	The school budget preparation process begins with the involvement of the budget development team.
	Person Responsible: School leaders and Site-Based Decision Making team members.
April 1	Completed school budgets should be submitted to the district administrator responsible for the consolidation of the organizational budget.
	Person Responsible: School leaders
April 15	The district administrator should submit the overall organizational budget to the superintendent of schools for review, along with suggested revisions prior to consolidation into a total district budget.
	Person Responsible: Associate Superintendent for Finance

(Continued)

(Continued)

Schedule	Procedure
May 15	The accepted budget for the entire school district should be prepared and ready for adoption in its final form.
	Person Responsible: Associate Superintendent for Finance and Superintendent
June 1	The superintendent of schools should have completed the review of the accepted budget in its final form.
	Person Responsible: Superintendent
Months of June/July	Budget workshops are scheduled for school board members.
	Person Responsible: Superintendent and School Board
No later than August 15	The district budget should be submitted to the local school board for public hearings and final approval. This final date will vary from district to district. However, the final approval date is typically prescribed by state law as any district and school budget must be approved prior to the expenditure of public funds.
	Person Responsible: School Board, Superintendent, and Associate Superintendent for Finance
No later than August 31	Budget adopted
	Person Responsible: School Board

The development and utilization of a budget calendar serves to assist in the formulation of an integrated plan of fiscal operations and further provides a means of communication between the various levels of the organization. Finally, the budget calendar effectively provides each administrator within the organization with the appropriate information and deadlines necessary to perform the duties associated with the budget development process.

The Budget Hearing and Defense

Many districts require school administrators, department directors, and other school personnel who are responsible for the development of budgets to formally meet and independently defend their budgets. This process can be quite stressful if the administrator has not properly and effectively prepared the budget in question. Preparation for the budget hearing and defense requires the school administrator to devise an interesting and informative manner of presenting the fiscal facts regarding the budget. This is often accomplished with the aid of visuals that better serve to present the necessary points and justifications associated with a budget. The school administrator must also comprehend the components of the budget (accounting codes and descriptors), have been intimately involved in the budget development process, and must further understand the reasons for the monetary requests that accompany the proposed budget. Some districts require the school administrator to meet with the superintendent of schools or a designee, and in some instances, a committee of supervisors or peers. In any case, the process typically includes the necessary justification of questioned budgetary items with final approval coming only after adjustments or revisions have been made to the proposed budget.

Finally, it is advised that the school administrator follow this useful adage: The best defense is a good offense. In other words, work hard at developing an effective budget, do the necessary homework associated with the budgetary tasks, and be prepared to expect the unexpected when defending the budget.

Final Thoughts

The effective school leader understands the importance of budgeting, especially as schools and school districts begin to realize that the function of a budget is more than mechanics and mathematics. The development of a school budget today requires strong leadership skills, a vision with a purpose, and an action plan for the future. The development of an effective school budget also necessitates teamwork, dedicated efforts, and proper coding. Budget development also demands budgetary applications whereby major budgeting considerations increase opportunities for all parties to play an active role in defining school issues and addressing problems, and as a result, generates appropriate decisions and solutions.

Effective leadership enables a school administrator to develop a budget that projects the school's vision and academic action plan. Moreover, the effective school leader informs the general public regarding the direction of the school program, and provides the framework for appropriate accounting and wise expenditure of educational dollars for the benefit of the students served. While no budget is ever perfect, proper visioning, regular planning, and continuous evaluation turns a common ledger of revenue and expenditures into a serious document of increased significance and relevance.

While building a school budget is never an easy task, it can provide the necessary framework to help make a school's vision a reality. With the institutionalization of the site-based decision-making model in our schools today, educational leaders have the opportunity and the obligation to engage the learning community in the budget development process by working collaboratively with all parties to incorporate visioning and planning as necessary components in better budgets for better schools. By applying proven budgeting theory and techniques, administrators today—working with an attitude of "all of us are smarter than any one of us"—can utilize budgetary applications in a manner in which the final budget compilation can positively impact the overall educational program and most important, increase the academic achievement of all students.

Discussion Questions

1. What is the purpose of the accounting code system?

2. How has the total quality movement and the site-based decision-making process impacted the development of budgets in public schools today?

3. Identify "players" in the budget-development process and explain how the notion "all of us are smarter than any one of us" can serve to ensure better budgets for better schools.

4. Who should be responsible for student enrollment projections—school district administration or school principals? Explain your answer.

5. How might the school budget applications detailed within this chapter serve the school administrator at the budget-defense hearing?

6. Why are certain budget allotments more restrictive than others? Explain your answer by providing examples.

7. You are now in the second semester of your first year as a school administrator, and the budget season is hastily approaching. You believe that your school enrollment has been rapidly growing over the previous three years. The associate superintendent for administration informs you that your budget allotment will be less for the upcoming fiscal year because the school district needs extra funds for a new facilities improvement effort. Your current enrollment is 815 students. Last school year, the enrollment was 796. The year prior, the enrollment was 779. Three years ago, the enrollment was 761. For previous years four, five, and six, student enrollment was 761, 757, and 752, respectively. How should you address the possibility of a decrease in your budgetary allotment? What methods would you apply and specifically utilize to resolve this issue in favor of your school at the upcoming budget defense hearing? Apply your answer(s) in writing.

8. Why is the incorporation and utilization of a budget calendar important to building an effective school budget?

Case Study Application 1: Shifting Paradigms With Changing Times

Note: This case study is a continuation of the one introduced in Chapter 4. The reader will recognize the characters portrayed and will further apply accounting codes to the budgetary allotments designated on pages 89–91 of Chapter 4 within the *PBHS Non-Prioritized Identified Needs* chart.

Part 4: The Budget—Coding the Budgetary Allotments

The Situation

Dr. Hector Avila, principal, and Ms. Abigail Grayson, assistant principal, at Pecan Bay High School sat down the next Tuesday afternoon with the SBDM committee to review the prioritized needs listing as related to the next fiscal year school budget. It was obvious that there were more needs than dollars at Pecan Bay High School. Dr. Avila thought to himself, "Isn't that always the case!" Nevertheless, the decisions had been made in what was considered the best interests of the students at PBHS. Dr. Avila was proud of the committee efforts. Ms. Grayson was more than impressed with the progress that had been made, and with how much she was learning from an outstanding instructional leader. While funding all the needs would be impossible based on the $100,000 allotment, the next step in the visioning, planning, and budgeting process was to integrate the needs with budgetary descriptors and accounting codes. This would be a learning experience for not only Ms. Grayson but for the entire SBDM committee. What Dr. Avila really appreciated about the site-based decision-making initiative was the fact that every aspect of the budget was being considered, assessed, evaluated, and approved in a public forum where all would recognize there were no hidden agendas or secret principal "slush" funds.

Following a short period of greetings and welcoming committee members to the conference room, the business of coding the differing needs began in earnest. Troy Allens, one of the initial opponents to the SBDM process and good friend of Ed Feeney, was present, smile on his face, and excited to be a part of a group who had bought into the concept of "all of us are smarter than any one of us!" Even old Ed was slowly, but surely, coming along and had even sat in on a SBDM meeting for Troy a few weeks ago when Troy had to take his daughter to a softball game.

Thinking It Through

Now that you have prioritized the differing needs at Pecan Bay High School and constructed an abridged action plan, it is time to consider all line-item accounts within the school budget in relation to the fund, function, object, subobject (utilize .00 for this exercise), organization, fiscal year, and program intent codes. Let's review from Chapter 1 the *Ten Steps to Budgeting Success* to determine what the committee has accomplished thus far: (1) determine the allotment, (2) identify any fixed expenditures, (3) involve all parties, (4) identify potential expenditures, (5) cut back as is necessary, (6) avoid any debts, (7) develop a plan of action, (8) set goals, (9) evaluate the budget, and (10) abide by the budget.

Where are you and your team in the ten-step process?

Take an opportunity to turn to Resource B: *Accounting Codes Reference Sheet.* Use this document to complete the Budget Spreadsheet exhibited on the next page by listing the correct accounting codes as associated with the prioritized needs previously selected. To assist you, an example indicating the proper accounting code for Health Services (Nurse or Clinic) has been provided and listed on the first row of the Budget Spreadsheet. Note that the description category of the Budget Spread Sheet is associated with the Function and Object code descriptors. Remember, accounting codes may vary from state to state and from district to district. The process utilized in this text serves only as an example. Seek your own state or school district version of the accounting code process.

Budget Development Spreadsheet

Fund	Function	Object/ Subobject	Year	Program Intent	Organization	Description	Total
199	33	6399.00	08	11	002	Health Services (Nurse)	$1000.00
							Grand Total	$

NOTE: This form also appears in Resource A.

Case Study Application 2: Requisition Season at Cover Elementary

Donna Arnold, assistant principal at Cover Elementary School, has been given the responsibility of serving as budget manager for the 2008–2009 school year. Donna has been an assistant principal at Cover for three years. She has really come to like the old school, the first one built in the school district well over 50 years ago. One of Donna's specified tasks associated with the role of budget manager is to review all campus requisitions that are submitted, and then assign the appropriate accounting codes. This evening, after a long day at school, Donna sits down and begins analyzing a stack of requisitions that were placed on her desk earlier that morning by her secretary. As she examines each requisition, she realizes how important it is that she learn the differing accounting codes in order to save time as she completes this particular task. While she thumbs through the stack of requisitions, she notes out loud what is being ordered and then attempts to speculate as to the appropriate code for entry in the fund account number blank.

Requisition #1: Janice Minsky wants to order the "director's cut" of the 1960 video production *Alamo*, starring John Wayne, to show to her Title I fourth-grade social studies class.

_____ __ ____ __ _____.____ __ ____ __ ____ __ _____

Requisition #2: Dolores Chavez needs one grand prize trophy and several ribbons for "placing," as well as certificates of achievement, for the Gifted and Talented students participating in the annual National Geography Bee.

_____ __ ____ __ _____.____ __ ____ __ ____ __ _____

Requisition #3: Henri Adams, librarian, requests several new book titles for the school library as the bilingual teachers strongly desire books in the native language of their Limited English Proficient students.

_____ __ ____ __ _____.____ __ ____ __ ____ __ _____

Requisition #4: Betty Sanchez, the school nurse, is demanding once again that she be permitted to attend the National Conference for Wellness Programs to be held in Chicago, Illinois.

_____ __ ____ __ _____.____ __ ____ __ ____ __ _____

Requisition #5: Julie Aikman wants a set of colored transparencies for her resource room to aid her students with visual-reading perception problems.

_____ __ ____ __ _____.____ __ ____ __ ____ __ _____

Requisition #6: Larry Nolton, building principal, is seeking to renew the subscriptions to *The Journal of Principal Leadership* for all of his administrative team members.

_____ — ____ — _____.____ — ____ — ____ — ____

Application Questions

1. Using Tables 6.6 through 6.10 within the chapter, as well as Resource B: *Accounting Codes Reference Sheet,* indicate the fund, function, object, subobject (utilize .00 for this exercise), fiscal year, program intent, and organization codes for each of the requisition submissions noted above. Place your answer in the blanks below each Requisition number. (Answers are provided at the conclusion of this chapter.)

Answers

Noted below are the answers to the activities in this chapter.

Answer to Form 6.1: Sample Requisition Form

199—36—6399.00—91

Answers to Special Activity 1 and 2: Utilizing Accounting Codes

#1   200—10—6300—002—23

#2   199—36—6399.00—91

Answers to Application Questions

Requisition #1:   199—11—6399.00—09—11—101

Requisition #2:   461—11—6399.00—09—21—101

Requisition #3:   219—12—6669.00—09—25—101

Requisition #4:   199—33—6411.00—09—11—101

Requisition #5:   199—11—6329.00—09—23—101

Requisition #6:   199—23—6329.00—09—11—101

7

Celebrating Success, Acknowledging Opportunities, and Ethical Leadership

Promise yourself to be too large for worry, too noble for anger, too strong for fear, and too happy to permit the presence of trouble.

—The Optimist's Creed, 1922

As we close, let us examine three final topics: (1) celebrating successes, (2) acknowledging opportunities for professional growth and development, and (3) recognizing the need for ethical and moral behavior in the leadership role.

Celebrating Success

School leaders must understand their impact on the school's culture. The leader establishes the tone for the school. In an era of increased outside accountability systems, stakeholders in schools are experiencing tremendous stress. Teacher attrition is the largest single factor determining the shortage of qualified teachers in the United States (Dove, 2004). Stress manifests itself with employees taking "mental health" days in order to flee the many sources of stress in their lives. Leaders must be cognizant of this underlying current in their schools.

Complainers are abundant in our society. At times they relish in their venting and in some instances in intimidating school employees. Educators often receive exponentially more complaints than they do compliments. Yet a major motivation for people entering this field is an intrinsic one—one of personal satisfaction for helping others (Ryan & Cooper, 2004). We all hold precious memories of those notes and conversations where appreciation was given for our efforts. There are times when we mentally recall these celebrations of success to help us cope with a current stress filled situation.

Ubben, Hughes, and Norris (2004) caution us not to underestimate the efficacy of public rewards of achievement. Effective organizations celebrate success. There are many terms of endearment for celebrating success among them are fradela, hullabaloo, hoopla, tadoo, wingding, and heehaw. As the leader of the school we must be the Director of Hullabaloo. We must set the tone of the school. We cannot shuffle this obligation to anyone else. We must lead in the establishment of a culture of appreciation for success.

Leadership in celebrating success can manifest itself in any number of ways. It is only limited by one's imagination. Leaders have led celebrations at their schools for achieving goals by performing out-of-character acts such as kissing a pig, shaving their heads, sitting on the roof, dancing in a pink tutu, doing an Elvis impersonation, and riding a Harley-Davidson through the gym. This type of manifestation of success celebration often brings with it the side benefit of positive local media attention to our schools. Sometimes as leaders we just have to let the stakeholders have a little fun at our expense. We do this because we know that school cultures that have an atmosphere of love and support for their stakeholders can accomplish miraculous transformations in student performance.

Celebrating success is not limited to public stunts. Celebrating success can also be private. A handwritten note of thanks can be worth a million dollars. Everyone, including the reader, treasures personal notes of gratitude. These notes are often tucked away and read again in moments of frustration or times of reminiscing. An eye-to-eye verbal compliment can reap a positive benefit to the recipient as well as to the giver. Compliments do not need to be lengthy; they only need

Figure 7.1　　Integrated Vision, Planning, and Budgeting

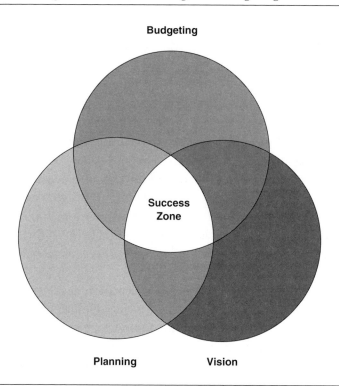

to be sincere. As a sidebar, leaders must know how to model accepting a compliment. We should not try to brush away the compliment by saying things like "It was nothing." Instead, we must honor the compliment-giver and say something like, "Thank you so much. I appreciate you recognizing my work and the work of my colleagues."

Celebrating success can manifest itself in many other ways: awards assemblies, bulletin boards, newsletter references, marquees, parking privileges, covering a class so a teacher can have a longer lunch, T-shirts, and any other positive idea you possess.

Opportunities to celebrate success will increase when you align your budget with your vision and planning. Figure 7.1 illustrates the alignment of these three factors. Vision, planning, and budgeting are represented by overlapping circles. The overlapping represents alignment of the processes. For example, the area where the budgeting circle and vision circle overlap is where the budgeting and vision processes are aligned. The areas where they do not overlap are opportunities for improving the alignment process.

The area labeled Success Zone is where all three processes are aligned. This is where leaders are seeking to take their schools. It is where the budget-vision-planning processes are fully aligned and integrated. The greater the alignment, the more the circles migrate toward the center of the figure and the larger the Success Zone becomes. Perfect alignment would manifest itself with all three circles stacked on top of each other with the Success Zone becoming a perfect circle.

As we lead our schools using the collaborative planning process to implement the integrated budget model, we will increase the size of the Success Zone which will, in turn, lead us to greater opportunities for success. Bathe your school with the celebrating of success as you lead the process to integrate the budget with the vision and planning. You just might reach Nirvana, that is, when your circles are completely stacked.

Celebration should be an all-inclusive process. Do not limit it to teachers and students. Include everyone—the custodians, bus drivers, cafeteria help, parent volunteers. A positive, optimistic, and supportive school culture increases energy and motivation, and this is contagious to all of our stakeholders (Deal & Peterson, 1999; Scheurich, 1998). Encourage teachers to help their students celebrate success as you help your charges celebrate success. Be the head cheerleader for your school, you might even get to wear the uniform!

Acknowledging Opportunities for Growth and Development

The work of schools since the early 1980s has become more complex and demanding. The immediate cause of this phenomenon, according to Elmore (2002), is quite simple. A powerful idea dominating policy discourse about schools stipulate that students must be held to higher academic achievement expectations and school leaders must be held accountable for ensuring that all students meet and exceed such expectations. This perspective and multiple others have subsequently dictated "numerous, simultaneous, and systematic changes in organizing, teaching, and administering schools" (Hoy & Miskel, 2005, p. 292). Such emerging viewpoints, demands, and expectations have dictated the absolute need for school leaders to be active participants in continuous and varied professional development opportunities.

For school leaders to be successful in any educational endeavor— whether it be envisioning school reform initiatives, planning programmatic changes, developing a school budget, or advancing opportunities for increased student achievement—we must understand that the once-standard, one-shot inservice workshop model is no longer acceptable. What we do know and what the research supports is that professional development must be entrenched in practice, research-based, collaborative, standards-aligned, assessment-driven, and accountability-focused procedures—all of which serve to increase the capacity, knowledge, and skills of administrators to improve their leadership practices and performances (National Staff Development Council, 2001). We must also recognize that student learning can only be enhanced by the professional growth and development of school leaders (Desimone, et al., 2002).

Staff development, like other facets of a school, must be data driven. Needs assessment surveys from the faculty analyzed in conjunction with data from other sources such as student achievement data will increase the effectiveness of the training resulting in increased performance of both the employees and the students.

An example of data-driven staff development occurred in a school that was having a high percentage of students who were not meeting with success in writing as measured by the state's assessment program. A review of the testing data by the SBDM committee revealed that this problem was evident throughout all the assessed grades. The planning committee surveyed the teachers and discovered that the writing teachers felt inadequately trained to teach writing within the parameters of the curriculum and assessment program of the state. They also discovered that writing was only a priority for the English teachers in the grades that were tested. Other teachers felt no ownership in teaching writing across the curriculum.

The committee conducted a review of possible writing workshops and selected one they deemed most appropriate for their students based on an analysis of the disaggregated achievement data. The committee also surveyed teachers throughout the district and developed a writing-across-the-curriculum plan that was supported by the faculty.

The SBDM committee ensured that these two strategies were incorporated in the school action plan. Funding was secured to bring in the writing consultants as well as to secure the required materials for the teachers. Likewise, the training received priority on the staff development calendar.

Referring back to Figure 7.1, we can see evidence of the alignment of the three elements of vision, planning, budget. Vision manifested itself in that the school's vision was to have all students meet with academic success. Planning occurred through data gathering, data analysis, and the needs prioritization conducted by the school's SBDM committee. Budgeting was present through the commitment of fiscal resources, time, and personnel. The writing project was definitely in the Success Zone. The data support this conclusion in that, three years later, the school's scores in writing had made significant increases going from significantly below state average to above state average.

The Leadership Role: Ethical and Moral Behaviors

Recent work by O'Donnell and Sorenson (2005) reveals that, as educational leaders, we face numerous dilemmas of differing dimensions on a regular basis. The best of leaders recognize these dilemmas as opportunities for doing what is right, not necessarily what is expedient. As school leaders, we have an obligation to set ethical and moral examples for the organizations we serve. Those leaders who do not honor integrity, those who fail to establish truth and who further negate moral reasoning are the same leaders who fail to inspire honesty and ethical practice in others. Such inappropriate behaviors in our business so often lead to moral abandonment, pure selfishness, and the ultimate in career derailment.

A few years ago, a Harris poll reported that 89% of workers and leaders surveyed believed it was important for leaders to be upright, honest, and ethical in their behaviors. However, only 41% indicated their current leader had such characteristics (Harris poll, *Business Week*, 1989). Such an indictment serves to underscore the need for character and ethical behavior in the school leadership business. Followers place their trust in a leader who models integrity and when leaders compromise their moral and ethical values, they risk losing the respect they so readily deserve (Nelson & Toler, 2002). What we do know about ethics is striking: "Ethics has to do with what leaders do and who leaders are" (Northouse, 2004, p. 302). While the daily pressures of life and career are often overwhelming, the effective school leader must remain an individual of committed character, integrity, and personal ethics. Leaders can ill afford to ignore strong moral and ethical margins, because the aforementioned stresses can compromise the decision-making processes, and when such occurs, a leader's character is terribly strained revealing flaws, cracks, and defects which in turn allow a leader to be susceptible to deception (lying and cheating), inappropriate behaviors (sexual affairs), and questionable or illegal actions (embezzlement), and a general lack of personal accountability

(Nelson & Toler, 2002). As a result, professional behavior, personal integrity, and appropriate ethical conduct must be the defining qualities of any leader. Nothing less will do. If trust and integrity serve as the paramount bond between school administration and faculty, what guidelines or principles should serve as the focal point to better ensure ethical conduct and moral leadership? Here are five targeted areas for serious leadership consideration.

1. Show respect—True leaders earn respect by showing respect for others. When leaders fail to respect followers, they fail to understand the main goal of leadership, which is leading. This may seem quaint, but effective leaders epitomize affirmation, listening, esteem, care, and concern—all inherently related to respect. Respect has been described by Northouse (2004) as granting credibility to the ideas of others and treating others in a way that makes them feel valued and competent.

2. Demonstrate integrity—Whatever qualities, skills, or talents a leader may possess, lacking integrity is an absolute flaw. Yukl (2001) advances the theory that leaders who demonstrate high levels of integrity are more credible, more open, more receptive to receiving bad news or negative feedback, and are less likely to be consumed with impressing their superiors at the expense of others.

3. Exhibit honesty—Honesty is best defined in relation to what it is not, what an effective leader cannot be: deceitful, untrustworthy, and fraudulent. The leader who exhibits honesty reveals a genuine honorableness in character and action.

4. Resist temptation—The moral and ethical strength of any school leader is often tested by the many temptations in life. Resistance is often accompanied by endurance. When a leader is close to temptation, a loss of perspective has occurred. Resisting temptation serves to make a school leader more respected, honest, and endearing to others who furthermore perceive the leader to be an individual who possesses the highest level of integrity.

5. Provide service—The effective school leader is one who is involved in servant leadership. The servant leader is one who is willing to empathize and understand by listening, by observing, and by assisting others within the learning community

(Greenleaf, 2002). Servant leadership provides for a level of tolerance by recognizing the strengths and talents of others when their weaknesses and mistakes may be more than obvious (DePree, 1997). Servant leadership can help others overcome their own weaknesses and mistakes by targeting those areas for personal and professional growth while at the same time emphasizing their not-so-apparent strengths and talents. In turn, followers are more likely to be just as tolerant of a leader when her or his mistakes are made, and when weaknesses are exhibited (Beckner, 2004).

Finally, we close with some serious advice for the educational leader who must always make appropriate decisions by upholding ethical behavior, even in an era when a general cynicism exists regarding the integrity of individuals in leadership positions, especially those leaders who actually espouse personal ethics and moral values. It would be well for all school leaders to consider and remember the following adage, as no words of advice could ring truer:

It's important that people know what you stand for
It's equally important that they know what you won't stand for.

—Mary Waldrop

Resource A

Selected Forms

Budget Development Spreadsheet

Fund	Function	Object Subobject	Year	Program Intent	Organization	Description	Total
						Grand Total	$

Strategy Page

Goal 1:

Objective 1:

Strategy 1:

Actions	*Responsibility*	*Timeline Start/End*	*Resources Human Material Fiscal*	*Audit (Formative)*	*Reported/ Documented*

Evaluation (Summative):

Resource B

Experiential Exercises

The Budgeting Codes Activity

Directions: Carefully read and assess each scenario presented and then refer to the Accounting Codes Reference Sheet, subsequently found within this appendix, to complete the activity. Fill in the blanks with the proper accounting codes. For the purpose of this exercise, utilize the current school year for fiscal year coding and .00 for the subobject code.

NOTE: Accounting Codes vary from state to state and from district to district. The codes utilized in Resource B are only one particular example.

1. Smyler Grogan, assistant principal at Desert Valley Elementary School, had been given the responsibility of budget manager and was working with the budget development team to prepare the school budget for the next fiscal year. In the course of the budget preparation process, Grogan was genuinely contemplating which accounting codes would best correlate with the budgetary decisions made by he and the team. He knew that the school's guidance counselor, Mrs. Vestal Umberger, needed a new filing credenza for her office. Desert Valley was built in 1962 and was the third elementary school in the district at the time; and Mr. Grogan realized that much of the furniture in Mrs. Umberger's office had never been replaced.

Fill in the blanks with the proper coding:

_____ — __ — __ — _____ . ___ — __ — __ — __ — __

2. Consuelo Estringel, principal at the Mission Hills Alternative Center for Education, was reviewing the monthly budget report when she realized that she had not budgeted for the additional $2,000 that would be needed to pay for the honorarium to be provided to the staff development presenter who was coming next week. Quickly, she began completing a district budget amendment form to ensure that the budgeted dollars would be available in the correct account. The presenter was a known expert in the area of teaching methodologies as associated with effective alternative school settings. Dr. Estringel finished the budget amendment, thus making certain that the appropriate funds were budgeted for this summer school program. She then called the presenter to verify his acceptance of the district contract.

Fill in the blanks with the proper coding:

_____ — ____ — _____ . ____ — ____ — ____ — _____

3. Tim Spedman, site-based committee chair at Western Ridge Middle School, was just finishing his lunch the other day when Letty Muñoz—the school secretary—came by and told Tim that he needed to provide her with an accounting code for a recent purchase he had made. Letty always had to track down Tim each time he spent money out of the school's activity account for items associated with the journalism department. She knew that Tim was an exceptional teacher, but he had to be more responsible when it came to keeping up with activity fund expenditures.

Letty, being quite frustrated at the moment, thought to herself: "This old school (the second middle school built in the district) is really getting to me!" She then told Tim that he needed to allocate funding for the copy machine that the department was leasing from the Whatacopy Shop. In fact, she bluntly told him to "finish that deviled-egg sandwich and get me those account numbers right away!"

Fill in the blanks with the proper coding:

_____ — ____ — _____ . ____ — ____ — ____ — _____

_____ — ____ — _____ . ____ — ____ — ____ — _____

4. Bayou Elementary School was the newest elementary campus in Pecan Grove Independent School District. It had just opened four months ago to accommodate the growing

population of students in the greater Hudston metropolitan area. The seven other elementary schools were highly rated according to the statewide accountability standards. Susan Dianes knew that she had a task on her hands as she assumed the role of the school's first principal. Nevertheless, Dr. Dianes had been a strong assistant principal for four years at Enchanted Path Elementary School and had been an outstanding special education teacher for seven years in a nearby school district. However, today, she had to work with the site-based team, and some difficult decisions had to be made.

Dr. Dianes had received word earlier in the week that the school budget was about to be cut in the area of student field trips. Student travel had become a school board issue, and starting next semester any new student travel requests would be denied. Dr. Dianes knew that the fourth-grade class always made a major end-of-the-year trip to Seaside Kingdom down on the coast. Monies must be encumbered now or any attempt next semester to fund the trip would be met with stiff resistance from central office administration, not to mention the school board.

Later that afternoon, Dr. Dianes and the site-base team met, and all agreed that funds must be amended from other budgetary accounts. Thus, Dr. Dianes and the team reviewed the budget, determined where the cuts would come from; and then Dr. Dianes completed the necessary budget amendment forms.

Fill in the blanks with the proper coding:

_____—____—_____.____—____—____—_____

Accounting Codes Reference Sheet

State education codes across the nation require that a standard fiscal accounting system be adopted by each school district. A major purpose of any accounting code structure is to ensure that the sequence of codes uniformly applies to all school districts. Utilize this coding structure when responding to the scenarios presented in Resource B: Experiential Exercises.

$$199—11—6399.00—001—08—11$$
$$1 \qquad 2 \qquad 3 \quad 4 \quad 5 \quad 6 \quad 7$$

1. Fund Code (500+)*

199 = General Fund

211 = Title I

219 = Bilingual Education

235 = Title IV

243 = Vocational Education

461 = Campus Activity Fund

2. Function Code (27)

11 = Instruction

12 = Instructional Resources and Media Services

13 = Curriculum and Staff Development

21 = Instructional Leadership (Instructional Specialist)

23 = School Leadership (Administration)

31 = Guidance Counseling and Evaluation Services

32 = Social Work Services

33 = Health Services (Nurse)

36 = Extracurricular (Athletics, Drama, Choir, Band)

51 = Maintenance and Operations (Custodial Supplies)

52 = Security

53 = Computers/Maintenance and Repair (Students/Teachers)

61 = Community Services

3. Object Code (35)

6100 = Payroll Costs

    6110 = Teacher and Other Professional Personnel

    6112 = Salaries for Substitute Teachers

    6118 = Professional Personnel/Extra Duty Pay

    6119 = Other Professional Services

    6121 = Paraprofessional Personnel/Extra Duty Pay

    6129 = Salaries for Support Personnel

6200 = Professional and Contracted Services

    6219 = Other Professional Services

    6239 = Contracted Services

    6249 = Maintenance and Repair

    6269 = Rentals/Operating Leases

6300 = Supplies and Materials

    6329 = Reading Materials

    6339 = Testing Materials

    6395 = Technology Supplies/Equipment Under $500

    6399 = General Supplies

6400 = Other Operating Costs

    6411 = Travel/Subsistence (Employees)

    6412 = Travel/Subsistence (Students)

    6494 = Transportation (Buses)

    6498 = Hospitality Expenses

6600 = Capital Outlay—Equipment

    6639 = Furniture and Equipment Over $5,000

    6649 = Furniture and Equipment Under $5,000

    6669 = Library Books

4. Subobject Code

This code is often used to delineate, for example, secondary-level departments. (For the purpose of the exercises and activities within this book, utilize .00 for the subobject code.)

5. Organization Code (School) (900)

    001–040 = High School Campuses

    041–100 = Middle School Campuses

    101–698 = Elementary School Campuses

    699 = Summer School Organizations

6. Fiscal Year Code

06 = 2006

07 = 2007

08 = 2008

09 = 2009

10 = 2010, etc.

7. Program Intent Code (13)

11 = Basic Educational Services

21 = Gifted and Talented

22 = Career and Technology

23 = Special Education

25 = Bilingual Education

26 = Alternative Education Placement (AEP) Services

30 = Title I (Schoolwide Project)

91 = Athletics

* The number in parenthesis represents the total number of differing accounting codes which might be utilized when developing a school budget. The codes listed within the Accounting Codes Reference Sheet are the most commonly utilized at the site level.

The Budget Development Project

The Budget Development Project provides the reader with a comprehensive examination of a fictitious school and school district. The school will be known as Mountain Vista Elementary School, and the district will be called Mesa Valley Independent School District.

Mesa Valley ISD serves a major suburban area just north of a large urban center. The school district has earned an outstanding reputation over the years for its strong academic and extracurricular programs, its effective school leadership, and its financial well being. The district's tax base, while more than adequate, remains most interestingly diverse with local revenues generated from the agribusiness industry, which includes pecan-growing, milk and dairy products, cotton farming, cattle ranching, as well as an infusion of high-tech industries that ultimately attracted the now-famous computer company, Styl-USA, Inc. With a diverse tax base also comes a diverse population with socioeconomic levels representative of the poor agribusiness workers, the medium income urban flight families, and the independently wealthy CEOs—all of whom now reside in what has become known as Technology Valley.

Mesa Valley Independent School District serves 17,502 students. The district has three high schools, five middle schools, and fifteen elementary schools. Mountain Vista Elementary School is the fifth oldest elementary school in the district with a population of 818 students enrolled for the 2008–2009 school year. Listed below are total student enrollments over the previous five school years.

School Year	Student Enrollment
2007–2008	831
2006–2007	845
2005–2006	850
2004–2005	826
2003–2004	808

The campus has a free and reduced lunch population of 82% and is thus considered a Title I schoolwide project. The average daily attendance is 90%. Mountain Vista has a unique student population ranging from high socioeconomic background to high poverty status. The school is also home to a large Limited English Proficient (LEP) population, since many of the families living within the attendance zone are legalized farm workers employed by the numerous agribusinesses.

Mountain Vista Elementary School houses grades Prekindergarten through Grade 5 with a student population which consists of 80% Hispanic, 10% White, 5% African American, and 5% Asian American. Gifted and Talented students make up 4% of the population, 5% of the student body is identified as Special Education, and 25% is served in the bilingual education program. Also, the school has forty-two teachers, one counselor, one nurse, one nurse assistant, one assistant principal, one instructional facilitator, one librarian, thirteen instructional aides, two clerical aides, one secretary, one attendance clerk, and one principal.

Each of the grade levels at Mountain Vista Elementary School has six sections of students with the exception of prekindergarten (two sections—one bilingual and one monolingual), Grade 2 (five sections), and Grade 4 (five sections). Every grade level has one section of bilingual students, one section of Special Education Inclusion-Monolingual students (excepting prekindergarten), with the remaining sections serving monolingual students. Each section of bilingual students at every grade level is served by one teacher and one instructional aide. The pre-kindergarten sections are served by one teacher and one instructional aide each. Finally, the special education students are served by two teachers and five instructional aides.

Mountain Vista Elementary School also employs half time, one Gifted and Talented teacher and one speech therapist, as well as a full-time physical education teacher, music teacher, and Title VI aide. There are four custodians and five food services employees that serve the school as well. Finally, both faculty and administration agree that Mountain Vista Elementary School is in need of a full-time campus diagnostician and hope to convince the superintendent during the budget defense hearing of this specified educational necessity.

The Mesa Valley Independent School District associate superintendent for finance has indicated that each elementary school will be provided a per-pupil campus budget allocation of $2,537 for the next school year. This allocation is to support the school's academic programs, salaries, any supplemental stipends ($1,800) for special education teachers, bilingual teachers, math and science teachers, testing coordinators, and head librarian, counselor, nurse, custodian, and grade-level chairs. Listed below in tabular form are the annual salaries of all school personnel.

Salaries

Mountain Vista Elementary School

Personnel Position	Salary per year $
Teachers, nurse, librarian	38,500
Principal	64,000
Assistant principal	56,000
Counselor	47,000
Diagnostician	48,000
Instructional facilitator	49,000
Speech therapist	44,000
Testing coordinator	42,000
Security officer	34,000
Secretary	25,000
Instructional and clerical aides	22,000
Nurse assistant	22,000
Custodian (head)	32,000
Custodians	25,000
Food services	9,500
Consultant(s) per day	1,500

Mountain Vista Elementary School has been having problems with reading achievement and consequently, low problem solving skills in the area of mathematics as measured by the State Assessment of Essential Skills (SAES). This problem encompasses most of the content areas since reading is the primary factor for academic success. The site-based committee believes that the promotion of literacy at school and within the community should be a campus priority. Other academic considerations are included within the proposed campus action plan for the next school year. However, a needs assessment and priority analysis has not been conducted in relation to the action plan. Identified, on subsequent pages, is the Mountain View Elementary School's Campus Action Plan (CAP).

Finally, the school has recently experienced a turnover in campus leaders. The prior principal replaced a strong and effective instructional leader who had gained the trust, confidence, and respect of the learning community. However, this principal—Mr. Belton Dwanes—had since retired after leading the school to the highest accountability rating according to the State Education Agency. Mr. Dwanes's replacement for the previous two years had been a less-than-effective instructional leader, and both he and his assistant principal had resigned to pursue other educational interests. During the two years after Mr. Dwanes's retirement, the instructional program at Mountain Vista Elementary School had suffered, and just this school year, Dr. Alma Villa and her assistant, John Steven Twollers, had assumed the roles of principal and assistant principal at the school. Both realized that they had their work cut out for them, but both were professionals with excellent credentials and reputations. Both leaders, after reviewing the campus Academic Achievement Indicator Report (AAIR), certainly understood the charge that had been issued to them by Dr. Leroy J. Thedson, the Mesa Valley ISD superintendent: "Turn Mountain Vista around and get those scores back on track. I expect all of your test groups and subpopulation scores to be at 80% and higher in the next two years!"

Directions: To best complete the Budget Development Project, the following format is suggested. Carefully read, in sequence, each information guideline along with supporting materials and then complete the noted tasks before moving on to the next set of instructions. Refer to, read, and follow Information Guideline #4 only after completing the first three directives and activities.

This particular project has been an extremely successful activity and is often considered the most popular aspect of our budget course teachings as it permits the prospective practitioner to gain significant insights and experiences into building a school budget.

While no clinical practicum can ever be as true to life as the on-site school experience, the processes detailed within the *Budget Development Project* are intended to present the reader and student of the budgeting process with a meaningful and relevant perspective that is as close as possible to the actual budgetary practices of a real school and school district.

1. Follow the *Sorenson-Goldsmith Integrated Budget Model,* as identified in Chapter 4, which showcases the eight components necessary to define and select the appropriate stakeholders, conduct a needs assessment, analyze the data presented, prioritize needs, set goals and objectives, and develop an action plan.

2. Review all of the information and data provided (including the Mountain Vista Action Plan and Academic Achievement Indicator Report) to determine if the information and data are being appropriately, effectively, and efficiently utilized. If not, make any and all necessary changes.

3. Develop a campus budget for Mountain Vista Elementary School by reflecting upon the budgetary applications detailed in Chapter 6. Your completed budget project should include a *descriptive narrative, programmatic identifiers,* a *mission statement, student enrollment projections,* an *analysis of the academic action plan,* a *needs assessment* and *priority analysis,* a *teacher/student distribution table,* a *faculty distribution table,* a *forecast of population* trends utilizing the *Cohort Survival Method,* any *above basic personnel requests and justifications,* an *allocation statement,* and a *distribution of funds table and narrative,* along with the *final budget compilation* utilizing accounting codes, descriptors, and dollar totals.

   –BEGIN THE BUDGET DEVELOPMENT PROJECT–

   Good luck and good visioning, planning, and budgeting!

4. Now, after completing Information Guides 1, 2, and 3, you may turn to the *Mesa Valley Independent School District Memorandum* found at the conclusion of Resource B. Remember, this memorandum is to be read and complied with only after you have completed the first three information guidelines.

MOUNTAIN VISTA ELEMENTARY SCHOOL

2009–2010
Campus Action Plan

SBDM Committee

Belinda Del Monte, preschool teacher

Karla Billingsly, Grade 1 teacher

Leslie Lovington, Grade 2 teacher

Dianna Sanchez, Grade 3 bilingual teacher

Barbara Axleson, Grade 4 Title I teacher

Susie Wigington, Special Education teacher

Randy Woodson, Chief of policy-community member

Jenda Minter, music teacher

Phyllis Canton, instructional aide

Suzan Rollins, P.T.A. president

Molly Corlioni, parent

Flo Cortez, parent

Lillie Eagleston, parent

John Steven Twollers, assistant principal

Dr. Alma Villa, Principal

MISSION STATEMENT

Mountain View Elementary School will provide a safe environment for all students by fostering productive citizens for a better tomorrow.

Goal I: Increase student achievement after a review and analysis of SAES data.

Objective 1: By student population—gender, ethnicity, educationally disadvantaged (At-Risk), and instructional setting teacher—develop strategies which will increase student achievement.

Strategy 1: Target specific instructional objectives.

Action(s) Implementation(s)	Responsibility Staff Assigned	Timeline Start/End	Resources (Human, Material, Fiscal)	Audit (Formative)	Reported/ Documented
Identify instructional areas of strength; areas needing improvement; and areas of weakness with regard to specific SAES objectives.	Principal and teachers	August 2009– May 2010	SAES English Language Arts Reading Objectives and Measurement Specifications booklet; SAES Mathematics Objectives and Measurement Specifications booklet; MVISD Curriculum Guides; Instructional Resource Center materials; teacher-made materials; SAES disaggregated data Mountain Vista SAES Booklet Time on Target criterion-referenced pretests	Disaggregated Data Information Sheets, SAES ATTACK skills worksheets, diagnostic and screening results, and lesson plans	Principal's office

Evaluation (Summative): All disaggregated student groups will obtain 80% or greater mastery on SAES.

Goal II: Provide a curriculum that addresses the basic skills to increase student academic performance.

Objective 1: Explore and implement programs that will increase overall student achievement.

Strategy 1: Continue current instructional programs.

Action(s) Implementation(s)	Responsibility Staff Assigned	Timeline Start/End	Resources (Human, Material, Fiscal)	Audit (Formative)	Reported/ Documented
Develop staff development programs for Grade 4 process writing. Enhance the reading program by implementing: ___ phonemic/phonetic instruction ___ increased reading time per day ___ learning centers ___ subgrouping ___ integrated units ___ reading styles inventories Continue cross grade-level planning during the first six-weeks of school.	Principal and teachers Director of Elementary Education	August 2009– May 2010	Integrated Reader library books and software; Phonetic Readers teaching resources; SOAR With Knowledge instructional materials; Maria Carlo Reading Styles Inventory; and teacher-made resources	Integrated Reader participation charts and printout reports, as well as lesson plans Teacher observation of student performance Principal visitation and participation in classroom	Principal's office; lesson plans, and library circulation records.

Evaluation (Summative): All disaggregated student groups will obtain 80% or greater mastery on SAES.

Goal II: Provide a curriculum that addresses the basic skills to increase student academic performance.

Objective 1: Explore and implement programs that will increase overall student achievement.

Strategy 1: Continue current instructional programs.

Action(s) Implementation(s)	Responsibility Staff Assigned	Timeline Start/End	Resources (Human, Material, Fiscal)	Audit (Formative)	Reported/ Documented
Continue the *On-To Math* program. Develop a math curriculum cross-referenced guide incorporating *On-To Math, Maxim Math,* and *Math This Way* instructional programs. Design math diagnostic tests to be administered in grades 1–5. Integrate science and social studies into the math instructional program with the extensive implementation of *SOAR With Knowledge.* Plan lessons to incorporate the *Living Science Center* into the instructional program at least twice each six weeks throughout the school year.	Principal, teachers, Resource Center coordinator, and the Director of Elementary Education	August, 2009– May, 2010	*On-To Math* and *Maxim Math* teaching resources, MVISD curriculum guides, library books, classroom libraries and readers, periodicals, newspapers, other reading materials, and teacher-made resources	Software printout reports, as well as lesson plans

Teacher observation of student performance

Principal visitation and participation in classrooms | Principal's office; lesson plans; and library circulation records. |

Evaluation (Summative): All disaggregated student groups will obtain 80% or greater mastery on SAES.

Goal III: Develop methods and strategies to assist "at-risk" students to achieve academic success.

Objective 1: Identify and serve students in "at-risk" situations in order that they obtain 80% or greater mastery on SAES.

Strategy 1: Extend learning opportunities and intervention programs for "at-risk" students.

Action(s) Implementation(s)	Responsibility Staff Assigned	Timeline Start/End	Resources (Human, Material, Fiscal)	Audit (Formative)	Reported/ Documented
Follow guidelines for identification of "at-risk" students as mandated by the State Education Agency and the MVISD At-Risk Plan.	Principal, teachers, counselor, instructional aides, and security officer	August 2009– May 2010.	Principal and counselor, At-Risk Coordinator, and the campus At-Risk committee	At-Risk Student Activity and Identification Sheets	Principal's office
Continue tutoring, counseling, special education, and 504 referral programs, and interagency involvement referrals.					
Enhance the student mentoring program between Grades 3 and 4 "at-risk" students and Grades PreK–2 "at-risk" students.					
Implement Title I compacts to encourage parental involvement and awareness, as well as increase student achievement and teacher responsibility.					

Evaluation (Summative): All disaggregated student groups will obtain 80% or greater mastery on SAES.

Goal III: Develop methods and strategies to assist "at-risk" students to achieve academic success.

Objective 1: Identify and serve students in "at-risk" situations in order that they obtain 80% or greater mastery on SAES.

Strategy 2: Offer parent training and information sharing opportunities.

Action(s) Implementation(s)	Responsibility Staff Assigned	Timeline Start/End	Resources (Human, Material, Fiscal)	Audit (Formative)	Reported/ Documented
Conduct a parent classroom orientation program during the first six weeks of the school year.	Principal, counselor, At-Risk coordinator and committee, and teachers	August 2009– May 2010	Newsletters, meeting notices, and parent survey and evaluation forms	Parent newsletters, parent training workshop notifications, parent classroom orientation "sign-in" sheets, and parent evaluation forms	Principal's office
Provide for a *Parent University* each school year.					
Survey parents to determine needs to be addressed during the *Parent University* program.			Child care, phone bank, and door prizes		

Evaluation (Summative): Parent training opportunities and orientations will be held in order that all disaggregated student groups will obtain 80% or greater mastery on SAES.

ACADEMIC ACHIEVEMENT INDICATOR REPORT

2007–2008

Campus Report

CAMPUS NAME: MOUNTAIN VISTA ES

DISTRICT NAME   MESA VALLEY ISD

CAMPUS NUMBER: 105

ACCOUNTABILITY RATING:

Exemplary

Recognized

<u>Acceptable</u>

Low-Performing

State Education Agency

District Name: Mesa Valley ISD
Campus Name: MOUNTAIN VISTA ES
Campus #: 105

Academic Achievement Indicator Report
2007–2008 Campus Performance
Accountability Rating: Acceptable

Total Enrollment: 831
Grade Span PreK–5
School Type: Elementary

Indicator:	State, %	District, %	Campus, %	African American, %	Hispanic, %	White, %	Asian American, %	Econ. Disadv., %
SAES % Passing								
Grade 3								
Reading	71.3	78.9	74.2	75.6	69.7	80.5	83.2	67.4
Math	74.6	79.2	73.8	65.7	61.7	84.2	86.3	63.7
SAES % Passing								
Grade 4								
Reading	78.7	81.0	70.7	70.2	61.5	78.6	81.2	60.9
Math	68.3	71.6	62.3	58.4	57.7	66.0	71.3	40.0
Writing	78.6	84.7	75.2	70.7	69.6	80.6	83.2	60.7
SAES % Passing								
Grade 5								
Reading	75.5	77.2	60.1	57.6	52.9	69.3	72.4	40.0
Math	77.3	78.0	67.3	58.6	47.6	70.2	73.5	47.2
Attendance	94.5	95.6	90.1	88.5	85.3	95.4	98.7	82.3

Student Information

Total Students: 831

Students by Grade:		
	Prekindergarten	32
	Kindergarten	124
	Grade 1	121
	Grade 2	102
	Grade 3	123
	Grade 4	105
	Grade 5	181
	Special Education	43

Retention Rates by Grade, %:

	State	*District*	*Campus*
Kindergarten	1.7	0.7%	2.2
Grade 1	4.7	3.9	5.1
Grade 2	1.7	0.7	1.9
Grade 3	1.1	0.6	1.3
Grade 4	0.9	0.7	1.2
Grade 5	0.8	0.3	0.9

Budgeted Operating Expenditure Information

	Campus	Pct.	District	Pct.	State	Pct.
Total Campus Budget	$2,108,247	100	$116,168,713	100	$12,711,996,407	100
By Function:						
Instruction	$1,486,314	70.5	$88,520,559	76.2	$9,559,421,298	75.2
Administration	$215,041	10.2	$8,596,486	7.4	$953,399,731	7.5
Other Campus Costs	$406,892	19.3	$19,051,668	16.4	$2,199,175,378	17.3
Budgeted Instructional Operating Expenditures by Program:						
Regular Education	$1,142,975	76.9		86.9		86.8
Special Education	$84,720	5.7		11.4		11.2
Title I Education	$219,974	14.8		15.0		14.9
Bilingual Education	$11,891	0.8		4.7		3.6
Gifted/Talented Ed.	$26,754	1.8		1.3		0.6

MEMORANDUM

Mesa Valley Independent School District   *Committed to Excellence in Education*

TO: Dr. Alma Villa, Principal
        Mountain Vista Elementary School and
        The Budget Team Members

FROM: Dr. Leroy J. Thedson, Superintendent of Schools

DATE: April 10, 2009

SUBJECT: Budgetary Constraints and Reductions

Due to the recent closure of the Mountain Stream Manufacturing Plant, a significant loss of district revenue has occurred. To ensure that the district budget and reserves remain solvent, all schools and departments are being asked to include a three percent (3%) reduction within their organizational budgets for the upcoming fiscal year.

Please note that the school district, along with the board of trustees, remain genuinely concerned about this momentary financial setback. However, also know that all areas of the district budget are being reduced, and expected revenue to be generated from the Valley Packing Company—which is scheduled to open within the next two years—will hopefully make up for this unexpected budgetary issue.

Your continued commitment to the students of this school district is most appreciated.

Resource C

Budgeting Checklist for School Administrators

School administrators have numerous tasks and responsibilities that are related to the school budget and other bookkeeping procedures. This checklist is intended to assist the school leader in mastering those tasks and responsibilities. Furthermore, it is anticipated that each of these checklist items will further serve to ensure a successful budgetary year as well as the overall success of those individuals involved in a most demanding yet essential budget development and bookkeeping process.

Bookkeeping Tasks and Responsibilities–

- ❑ Review all receipt books.
- ❑ Reconcile all bank statements monthly.
- ❑ Account for petty cash funds and reconcile monthly.
- ❑ Ensure each month that all checks have been signed with proper signatures.
- ❑ Visit on a regular (weekly) basis with the bookkeeping clerk regarding all budgetary considerations.
- ❑ Ensure that all bookkeeping personnel are bonded.
- ❑ Monitor all payments of bills and potential discounts for early or timely payments.
- ❑ Review any bookkeeping or budgetary issues that require your approval or signature. Examples include:
  - ❑ Checks
  - ❑ Purchase Orders
  - ❑ Financial Reports

□ Fundraising Requests
□ Amendments
□ Field-Trip Requests

Budget Manager Tasks and Responsibilities–

□ Examine and review the budget on a monthly basis.
□ Ensure that all requisitions that are prepared specifically list and identify the quantity ordered, proper accounting code(s), description of item(s) ordered, unit cost per item(s) ordered, sub-total, and grand totals are reflected on the requisition, originator is identified, and that the approval signature is noted.
□ During the requisition or budget season, ensure that all requisition forms are prepared by faculty and staff and submitted on a timely basis.
□ Ensure that all accounts have been properly audited by authorized outside accounting firms.
□ Update the faculty handbook annually regarding any fiscal and/or budgetary topics or issues.
□ Hold a faculty meeting prior to the budget development and requisition season to ensure that all parties understand the allocations provided as well as the proper procedures associated with requisition supplies, material, and all other budgetary considerations.
□ Develop a school academic action plan and integrate the plan with the school budget.
□ Review the different budget accounts each month. Do not allow for overexpenditures to roll forward from one month to the next.
□ Amend the school budget as is necessary and in accordance with the school academic or action plan.
□ Be aware of all district guidelines and deadlines associated with the school budget.
□ Spend all school funds wisely, appropriately, legally, timely, and with a student-centered approach/application.

Fundraising Considerations–

□ All fundraising must comply with local board policy or administrative regulations.
□ All fundraising requests must be monitored and approved prior to initiating any student-focused efforts.
□ What additional outside sources of revenue (adopt-a-school businesses, grants, foundation dollars, etc.) can further facilitate and enhance the budgetary allotment?

Site-Based Team and Budget Development–

- ❑ The budget development season begins each January by meeting with the site-based team to initiate discussions about issues and considerations that will impact the budget to be proposed for the next school year.
- ❑ Establish a budget calendar and begin regular meetings for the purpose of developing the school budget.
- ❑ Plan to spend the time necessary for proper budget development. In most cases, this will require several after school meetings and at least two half-day sessions and at least one full day meeting.
- ❑ Provide to the site-based team with the proper accounting codes and categories to begin the school budget development process.
- ❑ Establish with the team all revenue and expenditure targets for the next fiscal year budget. Enter all revenue and expenditure funds on the appropriate school form to be submitted to the district business department personnel.
- ❑ Examine any budgetary concerns that might have been problematic during the previous year budget cycle. Review the budget on an account by account basis.

Important Budgetary Questions–

- ❑ What is the budgetary allotment for the next fiscal year?
- ❑ What is the basis for the upcoming budgetary allotment?
- ❑ What is the projected student enrollment for next year and what is the per-pupil allotment?
- ❑ Are there any money or budgetary concerns or considerations that I should be aware of this week?
- ❑ Are any of our employees not following proper fiscal procedures as related to the budget or bookkeeping management, receipts, purchase orders, reimbursements, or financial reports to include bank reconciliation?
- ❑ Do any checks or purchase orders need approval and/or authorized signature?
- ❑ Are daily bank deposits being made?
- ❑ Are there any other items related to the school budget or bookkeeping procedures that we need to discuss or examine?
- ❑ What bookkeeping or budgetary improvements need to be made?
- ❑ When do I get a well-deserved vacation?

Resource D

State Departments of Education Websites

State education department home pages provide a vast amount of information related to educational topics and issues. In the case of this text, information gathered from different state education department websites, along with pertinent data, templates, and other relevant examples and materials are essential links to better understanding the school budgeting and planning processes. Each state department website can prove particularly useful when principals or other affected personnel are seeking specific accounting code formats as related to your state. In most instances, budgeting or school finance-oriented links should exist on the state education department home pages, and as a result, such should present opportunities for the viewer to download useful information. The best method for seeking specific budgetary topics, as related to your state, is to simply explore the home page and relatable links as time permits.

Listed below for your convenience is each of the 50 state education department websites. Remember that state education department home pages vary greatly in design and also in the amount of information provided. The best sites make available to the viewer the most up-to-date information and easy links to school budgeting and finance topics. School leaders should regularly take time to visit their state education department's website to review essential, if not critical, information related not only to budgeting and finance but to other educational issues as well.

State	Web site
Alabama	http://www.alsde.edu/
Alaska	http://www.eed.state.ak.us
Arizona	http://www.ade.state.az.us/
Arkansas	http://arkedu.state.ar.us/
California	http://www.cde.ca.gov
Colorado	http://www.cde.state.co.us/
Connecticut	http://www.state.ct.us/sde/
Delaware	http://www.doe.state.de.us/
Florida	http://www.fldoe.org
Georgia	http://www.doe.k12.ga.us/
Hawaii	http://doe.k12.hi.us
Idaho	http://www.sde.state.id.us/dept/
Illinois	http://www.isbe.state.il.us/
Indiana	http://www.doe.state.in.us
Iowa	http://www.state.ia.us/educate
Kansas	http://www.ksbe.state.ks.us/
Kentucky	http://www.education.ky.gov
Louisiana	http://www.doe.state.la.us/
Maine	http://www.state.me.us/education
Maryland	http://www.marylandpublicschools.org/msde
Massachusetts	http://www.doe.mass.edu
Michigan	http://www.mde.state.mi.us
Minnesota	http://www.education.state.mn.us
Mississippi	http://www.mde.k12.ms.us
Missouri	http://www.dese.state.mo.us
Montana	http://www.opi.state.mt.us
Nebraska	http://www.nde.state.ne.us
Nevada	http://www.doe.nv.gov
New Hampshire	http://www.ed.state.nh.us/
New Jersey	http://www.state.nj.us/education/
New Mexico	http://ped.state.nm.us
New York	http://www.nysed.gov/
North Carolina	http://www.dpi.state.nc.us/
North Dakota	http://www.dpi.state.nd.us
Ohio	http://www.ode.state.oh.us/
Oklahoma	http://sde.state.ok.us
Oregon	http://www.ode.state.or.us/
Pennsylvania	http://www.pde.state.pa.us
Rhode Island	http://www.ridoe.net

South Carolina	http://www.myscschools.com
South Dakota	http://www.doe.sd.gov
Tennessee	http://www.state.tn.us/education/
Texas	http://www.tea.state.tx.us/
Utah	http://www.usoe.k12.ut.us/
Vermont	http://www.state.vt.us/educ/
Virginia	http://www.pen.k12.va.us
Washington	http://www.k12.wa.us/
West Virginia	http://wvde.state.wv.us/
Wisconsin	http://www.dpi.state.wi.us/
Wyoming	http://www.k12.wy.us/

References

American Association of School Administrators (AASA). (1999). *Thinking differently: Recommendations for 21st century school board/superintendent leadership, governance, and teamwork for high student achievement.* Retrieved July 12, 2004 from http://www.aasa.org/issues_and_insights/governance/thinking_differently.htm

American Association of School Administrators. (2002). *Using data to improve schools: What's working.* Alexandria, VA: AASA.

Anderson, H. C. (1998). *Hans Anderson's fairy tales* (L. W. Kingsland, Trans.). Oxford: Oxford University Press.

Anderson, L. (1997). *They smell like sheep.* West Monroe, LA: Howard.

Arbatov, G., Morgan, P. M., & Nelson, K. L. (Eds.). (2000). *Reviewing the cold war: Domestic factors and foreign policy in the east-west confrontation.* Westport, CT: Praeger.

Banks, C. M. (2000). Gender and race as factors in educational leadership. In *The Jossey-Bass Reader on Educational Leadership* (pp. 217–256). San Francisco: Jossey-Bass.

Bannock, G., Baxter, R. E., & Davis, E. (1998). *Dictionary of economics* (6th ed.). London: Penguin.

Barth, R. S. (2001). *Learning by heart.* San Francisco: Jossey-Bass.

Beckner, W. (2004). *Ethics for educational leaders.* Boston: Pearson Education.

Berman, S. H. & Orion, D. K. (2003, March). The misdiagnosis of special education costs: District practices have no bearing, but medical and social factors accelerate spending. *School Administrator, 60,* 6+. Retrieved February 10, 2005, from Questia data base, http://www.questia.com

Birrup, P. E., Brimley, V., Jr., & Garfield, R. R. (1999). *Financing education: In a climate of change* (7th ed.). Boston: Allyn and Bacon.

Blumberg, A. and Greenfield, W. D. (1986). *The effective principal.* Boston: Allyn and Bacon.

Borja, B. R. (2005). Ethics issues snare school leaders. *Education Week, 24*(18), 1–4.

Bracey, G. W. (2002). *The war against America's public schools: Privatizing schools, commercializing education.* Boston: Allyn and Bacon.

Brewer, E. W., Achilles, C. M., Fuhriman, J. R. & Hollingsworth, C. (2001). *Finding funding: Grant writing from start to finish, including project management and internet use* (4th ed.). Thousand Oaks, CA: Corwin.

Brimley, V., Jr. & Garfield, R. (2002). *Financing education in a climate of change* (8th ed.). Boston: Allyn and Bacon.

Brimley, V., Jr., & Garfield, R. R. (2005). *Financing education in a climate of change* (9th ed.). Boston: Pearson Education.

Castallo, R. T. (Ed.), Fletcher, M. R., Rossetti, A. D. & Sekowski, R. W. (1992). *School personnel administration: A practitioner's guide.* Boston: Allyn and Bacon.

Castetter, W. B. (1996). *The human resource function in educational administration.* Englewood Cliffs, NJ: Prentice-Hall.

Cizek, G. J. (1999). *Cheating on tests: How to do it, detect it, and prevent it.* Mahwah, NJ: Lawrence Erlbaum.

Clover, C., Jones, E., Bailey, W., & Griffin, B. (2004). Budget priorities of selected principals: Reallocation of state funds. *NASSP Bulletin, 88*(640), 69–79.

Colorado Literacy Research Institute (2001). *Facts & figures from the Colorado literacy initiative, 5*(4).

Columbia World of Quotations, The. New York: Columbia University Press, 1996. Retrieved May 15, 2005, from http://www.bartleby.com/66

Congressional Quarterly (2000). *Where we stand: A commentary on public education and other critical issues.* Washington, DC: Author.

Cooper, T. L. (1998). *The responsible administrator: An approach to ethics for the administrative role.* San Francisco: Jossey-Bass.

Council of Chief State School Officers. (1996). *Interstate school leaders licensure consortium: Standards for school leaders.* Washington, DC: Author.

Covey, S. R. (1990). *The seven habits of highly effective people.* New York: Simon and Schuster.

Cuban, L. (1988). *The managerial imperative and the practice of leadership in schools.* Albany: State University of New York Press.

Daresh, J. C., (2001). *Beginning the principalship: A practical guide for new school leaders.* Thousand Oaks, CA: Corwin.

Dayton, J. (2002). Three decades of school funding litigation: Has it been worthwhile and when will it end? *School Business Affairs,* May 2002, pp. 7–9.

Deal, T. E. & Kennedy, A. A. (1982). *Corporate Cultures: The rites and rituals of corporate life.* Reading, MA: Addison-Wesley.

Deal, T. E. & Peterson, K. D. (1990). *The principal's role in shaping school culture.* Washington, DC: U.S. Department of Education, Office of Educational Research and Improvement.

Deal, T. E. & Peterson, K. D. (1999). *Shaping school culture.* San Francisco: Jossey-Bass.

DePree, M. (1997). *Leading without power: Finding hope in serving community.* San Francisco: Jossey-Bass.

Desimone, L. M., Porter, A. C., Garet, M. S., Yoon, K. S., and Briman, B. F. (2002). *Educational evaluation and policy analysis, 24*(2), 81–112.

Dorsch, N. G. (1998). *Community collaboration and collegiality in school reform.* Albany: State University of New York Press.

Doud, J. & Keller, E. (1998). *A ten-year study: The K-8 principal in 1998.* Alexandria, VA: National Association of Elementary School Principals.

Dove, M. K. (2004). Teacher attrition: A critical American and international education issue. *Delta Kappa Gamma Bulletin, 71*(1), 8–15.

Dyer, J. (2000). *The perpetual prisoner machine: How America profits from crime.* Boulder, CO: Westview.

Earl, L. (1995). Moving from the political to the practical: A hard look at assessment and accountability. *Orbit, 26*(2), 61–63.

Earl, L. & Katz, S. (2005). Painting a data-rich picture. *Principal Leadership* 5(5), 16–20.

Edmonds, R. R. (1979). Effective schools for the urban poor. *Educational leadership* 37(2), 15–24.

Elmore, R. F. (2002). *Bridging the gap between standards and achievement.* Washington, DC: Albert Shanker Institute.

Feldman, S. (2000). A blank check. Retrieved September 8, 2005 from, http://www.aft.org

Fisher, L., Schimmel, D. & Kelly, C. (1999). *Teachers and the law.* New York: Addison Wesley Longman.

Fowler, W. J., Jr. (1990). *Financial accounting for local and state school systems.* Washington, DC: U.S. Department of Education [Online]. Retrieved August 3, 2004, from http://nces.ed.gov

Fullan, M. G. (2001). *The new meaning of educational change.* New York: Teachers College Press.

Fullan, M. G. & Miles, M. (1992). Getting reform right: What works and what doesn't. *Phi Delta Kappan, 73*(10), 745–752.

Fullan, M. G. with Stiegelbauer, S. (1991). *The new meaning of educational change.* New York: Teachers College Press.

Funkhouser, C. W. (1999). *Education in Texas. Policies, practices, and perspectives* (9th ed.). Scottsdale, AZ: Gorsuch Scarisbrick.

Garner, C. W. (2004). *Education finance for school leaders: Strategic planning and administration.* Upper Saddle River, NJ: Pearson Education.

Garza C. L. (2005, January 16). Test-score swings draw scrutiny. *Fort Worth Star-Telegram,* Retrieved February 10, 2005, from http://www.dfw.com/mld/startelegram/news/local/10660418.htm

Godwords Theology and Other Good Stuff (n.d).[Online]. Is 99.9 percent good enough? (n.d.). Retrieved Feb. 11, 2005, from www.godwords.org/stories/99percent.html

Gonzales, G., Hamilton, L., & Stecher, B. (2003). *Working smarter to leave no child behind: Practical insights for school leaders.* Santa Monica, CA: Rand.

Gorton, R., Schneider, G., & Fisher, J. (1988). *Encyclopedia of school administration and supervision.* Phoenix, AZ: Oryx.

Governmental Accounting Standards Board (2001). *Codification of governmental accounting and financial reporting standards.* Norwalk, CT: Author.

Greenleaf, R. K. (2002). *Servant leadership: A journey into the nature of legitimate power and greatness.* Mahwah, NJ: Paulist Press.

Guthrie, J. W., Garms, W. I. & Pierce, L. C. (1988). *School finance and educational policy: Enhancing educational efficiency, equality and choice* (2nd ed.). Boston: Allyn and Bacon.

Hack, W. G., Candoli, I. C. & Ray, J. R. (2001). *School business administration: A planning approach* (7th ed.). Boston: Allyn and Bacon.

Hadderman, M. (2002). School-based budgeting. *Teacher Librarian, 30*(1), pp. 27–30.

Harris poll, reported in *Business Week,* May 29, 1989, p. 29.

Harris, S. (2004). Strategies to meet the challenge of the age of accountability. *Insight, 18*(3), 25–28.

Herman, J. J. & Herman, J. L (2001). *School-based budgets: Getting, spending, and accounting.* Lanham, MD: Scarecrow.

Holcomb, E. L. (2004). *Getting excited about data: Combining people, passion and proof to maximize student achievement* (2nd ed.). Thousand Oaks, CA: Corwin.

Honawar, V. (2001, May 10). Montgomery seeks test invalidation. *The Washington Times,* p. 3. Retrieved February 10, 2005, from Questia data base, http://www.questia.com

Hopkins, D. and West, M. (1994). Teacher development and school improvement: An account of improving the quality of education for all (IQEA) project. In D. R. Wallings (Ed.), *Teachers as Leaders: Perspectives on the professional development of teachers* (pp. 179–199). Bloomington, IN: Phi Delta Kappa.

Hoy, W. K. & Miskel, C. G. (2005). *Educational administration: Theory, research, and practice.* Boston: McGraw-Hill Higher Education.

Hughes, R. L., Ginnett, R. C. & Curphy, G. J. (2002). *Leadership: Enhancing the lessons of experience.* Columbus, OH: McGraw-Hill Higher Education.

Hylbert, A. (2002). The effects of the property tax extension limitation law upon revenue grow, bonded debt, and school business leader perceptions. *The Journal of School Business Management, 14*(2), 9–14.

Iger, A. L. (1998). *Music of the golden age, 1900–1950 and beyond: A guide to popular composers and lyricists.* Westport, CT: Greenwood.

Johnson, R. S. (2002). *Using data to close the achievement gap: How to measure equity in our schools* (2nd ed.). Thousand Oaks, CA: Corwin.

Jones, T. H. (1985). *Introduction to school finance: Technique and social policy.* New York: Macmillan.

Jones, T. H. & Amalfitano, J. L. (1994). *America's gamble: Public school finance and state lotteries.* Lancaster, PA: Technomic.

Kemerer, F. R. & Walsh, J. (2005). *The educator's guide to Texas school law* (6th ed.). Austin: University of Texas Press.

Kilmann, R. H., Saxton, M. J. & Serpa, R. (1985). Introduction: Five key issues in understanding changing culture. In R. H. Kilmann, M. J. Saxton & R. Serpa (Eds.), *Gaining control of the corporate culture* (pp. 1–16). San Francisco: Jossey-Bass.

Laffee, S. (2002, December). Data-driven districts. *The School Administrator, 59,* 6–15.

LaMorte, M. W. (2005). *School law: Cases and concepts.* Boston: Pearson Education.

Leithwood, K. (1990). The principal's role in teacher development. In B. Joyce (Ed.) *Changing school culture through staff development: 1990 yearbook of the Association for Supervision and Curriculum Development* (pp. 71–90). Alexandria, VA: ASCD.

Levin, H.M. (1991). Cost-effectiveness at quarter century in chapter 8: Evaluation and education at quarter century, *Ninetieth Yearbook of the National Society for the Study of Education, Part II.* Chicago, IL: University of Chicago Press.

Linder, D. (n.d.). Regulation of obscenity and nudity. Retrieved September 6, 2004, from Exploring Constitutional Conflicts Web site: http://www .law.unkc.edu/faculty/projects/ftrials/conlaw/obscenity.htm

LoBuglio, S. (2001, March). The annual review of adult learning and literacy. *In time to reframe politics and practices in correctional education* (2, chap. 4). National Center for the Study of Adult Learning and Literacy. Retrieved February 24, 2005, from http://ncsall.gse.harvard.edu/ann_rev/v012_ 4.html

Maeroff, G. I. (1994). On matters of body and mind: Overcoming disincentives to a teaching career. In D. R. Walling (Ed.), *Teachers as leaders: Perspectives on the professional development of teachers* (pp. 45–57). Bloomington, IN: Phi Delta Kappa.

Malen, B., Ogawa, R. T. & Kranz, J. (1990). Evidence says site-based management hindered by many factors. *The School Administrator,* February 1990, p. 32.

McCloskey, W., Mikow-Porto, V. & Bingham, S. (1998). Reflecting on progress: Site-based management and school improvement in North Carolina. (ERIC Document Reproduction Service ED 421766)

Murphy, J. & Shipman, N. J. (1998). *The interstate school leaders licensure consortium: A standards-based approach to strengthening educational leadership.*

Paper presented to the annual conference of the American Educational Research Association, San Diego, CA.

Mutter, D. W. & Parker, P. J. (2004). *School money matters: A handbook for principals.* Alexandria, VA: Association for Supervision and Curriculum Development (ASCD).

Nash, R. J. (1996). *"Real world" ethics: Frameworks for educators and human service professionals.* New York: Teachers College Press.

National Association of Secondary School Principals. (2001). *Priorities and barriers in high school leadership: A survey of principals.* Reston, VA: National Association of Secondary School Principals.

National Center for Education Statistics. (2005a) [Online]. Retrieved February 9, 2005, from http://nces.ed.gov/forum/pdf/nces_financial_handbook_pdf

National Center for Educational Statistics (2005b). [Online]. Table 5—Student membership and current expenditures per pupil in membership for public elementary and secondary schools, by function, state, and outlying areas: School year 2002–03. (2005). Retrieved June 15, 2005, from http://nces.ed.gov/ccd/pubs/npefs03/table_5.asp?popup=1

National Center for Education Statistics. (2005c) [Online]. Retrieved June 16, 2005, from http://nces.ed.gov

National Conference of State Legislatures. (2003a). State budget and tax actions 2003. July.

National Conference of State Legislatures. (2003b). Fiscal storm shows signs of subsiding, November.

National Policy Board for Educational Administration (NPBA). (2001). *Advanced programs in educational leadership for principals, superintendents, curriculum directors, and supervisors.* Washington, DC: National Policy Board for Educational Administration.

National Policy Board for Educational Administration (NPBA). (2002). *Instructions to implement standards for advanced programs in educational leadership for principals, superintendents, curriculum directors, and supervisors.* Arlington, VA: National Policy Board for Educational Administration.

National Staff Development Council. (2001). *Standards for staff development* (Rev. Ed.). Oxford, OH: Author. Available at www.nsdc.org/educator index.htm

Nelson, A. & Toler, S. (2002). *The five secrets to becoming a leader.* Ventura, CA: Regal Books.

No Child Left Behind Act. (2001). *Action plan components.* Washington, DC: Author.

Northouse, P. G. (2004). *Leadership: Theory and practice.* Thousand Oaks, CA: Sage.

Norton, M. S. (2005). *Executive leadership for effective administration.* Boston, MA: Pearson Education.

Odden, A. & Archibald, S. (2001). *Reallocating resources: How to boost student achievement without asking for more.* Thousand Oaks, CA: Corwin.

Odden, A. & Wohlsletter, P. (1995). Making school-based management work. *Educational Leadership, 52*(5), 32–36.

O'Donnell, L. & Sorenson, R. D. (2005). *How sex and money ruined Dr. Ed U. Kator's career.* Manuscript submitted for publication.

Office of Management and Budget (2005). *Preventing embezzlement.* Washington, DC: Author.

Ogawa, R. & Bossert, S. (1995). Leadership as an organizational quality. In *The Jossey-Bass Reader on Educational Leadership* (pp. 38–58). San Francisco: Jossey-Bass.

Oliva, P. (2005). *Developing the curriculum* (6th ed.). Boston: Pearson.

Osborne, J., Barbee, D. & Suydam, J. A. (1999). FBI asked to examine CCISD. *Corpus Christi Caller-Times.* Retrieved June 17, 2005, from http://www .caller2.com/1999/october/06/today/local_ne/1147.html

O'Shea, M. R. (2005). *From standards to success: A guide for school leaders.* Alexandria, VA: Association for Supervision and Curriculum Development (ASCD).

Ovsiew, L. & Castetter, W. B. (1960). *Budgeting for better schools.* Englewood Cliffs, NJ: Prentice-Hall.

Park, J. (2004). *School finance.* Education Week. [Online]. Retrieved July 9, 2004, from http://www.edweek.org

Peterson, S. (2001). *The grantwriter's internet companion: A resource for educators and others seeking grants and funding.* Thousand Oaks, CA: Corwin.

Phi Delta Kappa (1989). *Enrollment projections.* Bloomington, IN: Author.

Ramsey, R. D. (2001). *Fiscal fitness for school administrators: How to stretch resources and do even more with less.* Thousand Oaks, CA: Corwin.

Rebora, A. (2004, July 28). No child left behind. *Education Week on the Web,* Retrieved August 6, 2004, from http://edweek.org/context/topics/ issuespage.cfm?id=59

Reschovsky, A., & Imazeki, J. (2000, October). *Achieving educational adequacy through school finance reform.* CPRE Research Report Series RR-045. Philadelphia, PA: Consortium for Policy Research in Education.

Roe, W. H. (1961). *School business management.* New York: McGraw-Hill.

Ryan, K. & Cooper J. (2004). *Those who can teach* (10th ed.). Boston: Allyn and Bacon.

Sergiovanni, T. J., Kelleher, P., McCarthy, M. M. & Wirt, F. M. (2004). *Educational governance and administration.* Boston: Pearson Education.

Seyfarth, J. T. (2005). *Human resources management for effective schools.* Boston: Pearson Education.

Shipman, N. J., Topps, B. W., & Murphy, J. (1998). *Linking the ISLLC standards to professional development and re-licensure.* Paper presented to the annual conference of the American Educational Research Association, San Diego, CA.

Sorenson, R. D. & Goldsmith, L. M. (2004). *The budget-vision relationship: Understanding the interwoven process.* Paper presented at the annual Texas Association of Secondary School Principals New Principals Academy, Trinity University, San Antonio, Texas, July 8.

Stein, J. (Ed.). (1967). *The Random House dictionary of the English language* (Unabridged ed.). New York: Random House.

Swanson, A. D. & King, R. A. (1997). *School finance: Its economics and politics* (2nd ed.). New York: Longman.

Taylor, B. O. (2002, January). The effective schools process: alive and well. *Phi Delta Kappan* 83. Retrieved July 27, 2004, from http://web2.epnet.com/citation.asp

Thompson, D. C. & Wood, R. C. (1998). *Money and schools: A handbook for practitioners.* Larchmont, NY: Eye on Education.

Thompson, D. C. & Wood, R. C. (2001). *Money and schools.* Larchmont, NY: Eye on Education.

Thompson, D. C., Wood, R. C. & Honeyman, D. (1994). *Fiscal leadership for schools: Concepts and practices.* New York: Longman.

Ubben, G., Hughes, L., & Norris, C. (2004). *The principal: Creative leadership for excellence in schools* (5th ed.). New York: Pearson.

U.S. Office of Education (2003). *Financial accounting for local and state systems handbook.* Washington, DC: Author.

Universality of the golden rule in the world religions [The]. (n.d.). Retrieved July 27, 2004, from http://www.teachingvalues.com/goldenrule.html

Vail, K. (1998). Eleven ways to make money: When traditional funding isn't enough, many school districts become entrepreneurs. *American School Board Journal* 6, 30–31.

Vail, K. (1999, February). Insert coins in slot: School vending machines generate funds—and controversy. *American School Board Journal* 28.

Walton, M. (1986). *The Deming management method.* New York: Perigee.

Webb, L. D. (2006). *The history of American education: A great American experience.* Upper Saddle River, NJ: Pearson Education.

Webb, L. D. & Norton, M. S. (2004). *Human resources administration: Personnel issues and needs in education.* Upper Saddle River, NJ: Prentice-Hall.

Wells, J. T. (2002, September). Billing schemes, part 3: Pay-and-return invoicing. *Journal of Accountancy* 194, 96–98.

Wilkins, A. L. & Patterson, K. J. (1985). Five steps for closing culture-gaps. In R. H. Kilmann, M. J. Saxton & R. Serpa (Eds.), *Gaining control of the corporate culture* (pp. 351–369). San Francisco: Jossey-Bass.

Will, G. (2005, February 17). These bones protected by muscle. *Abilene Reporter-News,* p. 4AA.

Williams, G. W. (2004). *Activity fund accounting.* Paper presented at the Annual Meeting of TASSP New Principals Academy, Southern Methodist University, July 10, 2004.

Wohlstetter, P. & Buffett, T. M. (1992). Promoting school-based management: Are dollars decentralized too? In A. R. Odden (Ed.), *Rethinking school finance: An agenda for the 1990s* (pp. 128–165). San Francisco: Jossey-Bass.

Yeagley, R. (2002). A forum for becoming data savvy. *The School Administrator* 59(11), 13.

Young, I. P. & Castetter, W. B. (2003). *The human resource function in educational administration* (8th ed). Englewood Cliffs, NJ: Prentice-Hall.

Yukl, G. A. (2001). *Leadership in organizations* (4th ed). Englewood Cliffs, NJ: Prentice-Hall.

Index

**CORWIN
PRESS**

The Corwin Press logo—a raven striding across an open book—represents the union of courage and learning. Corwin Press is committed to improving education for all learners by publishing books and other professional development resources for those serving the field of PreK–12 education. By providing practical, hands-on materials, Corwin Press continues to carry out the promise of its motto: **"Helping Educators Do Their Work Better."**